THE SHORT PARLIAMENT (1640) DIARY
OF SIR THOMAS ASTON

THE SHORT PARLIAMENT
(1640) DIARY
OF SIR THOMAS ASTON

edited by
JUDITH D. MALTBY

CAMDEN FOURTH SERIES
VOLUME 35

LONDON
OFFICES OF THE ROYAL HISTORICAL SOCIETY
UNIVERSITY COLLEGE LONDON
GOWER STREET WC1E 6BT
1988

© 1988 Royal Historical Society

British Library Cataloguing in Publication Data

Aston, *Sir* Thomas, *1600–1646*
   The short Parliament (1640) diary of Sir
   Thomas Aston.—(Camden fourth series: v.35)
   1. England and Wales, Parliament, House
of Commons, 1640
   I. Title   II. Maltby, Judith D.   III. Series
   328.42′072

   ISBN 0–86193–116–5

Printed and bound in Great Britain by
Butler & Tanner Ltd, Frome and London

CONTENTS

ACKNOWLEDGEMENTS

My interest in Sir Thomas Aston pre-dates theovery of his diary of the Short Parliament. It was while pursuing Aston as a defender of the Book of Common Prayer and episcopacy that I learned from the Cheshire archivist, Mr Brian Redwood, that his descendants still retained in their possession a great number of Aston manuscripts.[1] I received permission from the family, now named Talbot, to come and look at their papers, which included Sir Thomas' Short Parliament diary. My debt of gratitude is very great to Mr Howard Talbot—not only for his permission to prepare an edition of the diary for publication, but also for his kindness, and that of his family, during my visits to Aston Lodge. I am grateful too for his continued interest in and help with my research on Aston as a lay defender of the Church of England.

I would also like to express my gratitude to the Principal and Fellows of Newnham College, Cambridge (particularly the Fellows in History), for electing me to a Research Fellowship which provided the financial and moral support to undertake this project. Support was also received for research expenses from the Archbishop Cranmer Fund and the Political Science Fund, both administered by the Faculty of History. I am grateful also for the patience and helpfulness of Mr Brian Redwood and the staff of the Cheshire Record Office as well as of the History of Parliament Trust. My debt is large, too, to the work of Professor Esther Cope who edited the previously known texts of the Short Parliament. My task would have been immeasurably more difficult but for her work. I have benefited greatly from the guidance of a number of individuals in the preparation of this edition: Professor Geoffrey Elton, Dr Sheila Lambert, Dr Margaret and Dr Peter Spufford, and especially Dr John Morrill and Mrs Dorothy Owen. My debt is particularly great to Mrs Owen, Keeper of the Cambridge University Archives not only for her expert and scholarly guidance, but also for the immense generosity she has shown with her time. Although it has become commonplace to say at this point that all remaining errors are one's own, it nevertheless remains true.

Newnham College,
Cambridge

---

[1] There are several volumes of Aston Manuscripts in the British Library's Additional Manuscripts (B.L. Add. Mss. 36913–19).

ABBREVIATIONS

AC	J. and J. A. Venn, eds., *Alumni Cantabrigienses*, 4 vols. (Cambridge, 1922–27).
AO	J. Forster, ed., *Alumni Oxonienses*, 4 vols. (Oxford, 1891–92).
BCP, 1559	John Booty, ed., *The Book of Common Prayer 1559* (Washington, D.C., 1976).
B.L.	British Library, London.
Cardwell, *Synodalia*	Edward Carwell, ed., *Synodalia*, 2 vols. (Oxford, 1842).
C.D. 1628	Robert C. Johnson, *et al.*, eds., *Commons Debates 1628*, 6 vols. (New Haven, 1977).
C.D. 1629	W. Notestein and F. H. Relf, eds., *Commons Debates 1629* (Minneapolis, 1921).
C.J.	*Journals of the House of Commons* (London, 1803–).
Cope	Esther Cope and Willson Coates, eds., *Proceedings of the Short Parliament 1640* (Camden 4th ser. xix, 1977).
CSPD	*Calendar of State Papers: Domestic Series* (London, 1857–).
D'Ewes (Notestein)	W. Notestein, ed., *The Journal of Sir Simonds D'Ewes from the Beginning of the Long Parliament to the Opening of the Trial of the Earl of Strafford* (New Haven, 1923).
DNB	*The Dictionary of National Biography.*
Fletcher, *Sussex*	Anthony Fletcher, *A County Community in Peace and War: Sussex 1600–1660* (London, 1975).
Foedera	T. Rymer and R. Sanderson, eds., *Foedera, conventiones, literae et cuiuscunque generis acta publica*, 20 vols. (London, 1704–32).
Gruenfelder, 'Short Parliament'	John Gruenfelder, 'The Election to the Short Parliament, 1640', *Early Stuart Studies*, Howard Reinmath, ed. (Minneapolis, 1970).

Hirst	Derek Hirst, *The Representative of the People?* (Cambridge, 1975).
H.M.C.	Historical Manuscripts Commission.
Keeler	Mary Keeler, *The Long Parliament, 1640–41* (Philadelphia, 1954).
Life	Edward Hyde, earl of Clarendon, *Life of Edward Earl of Clarendon* (London, 1759).
L.J.	*Journals of the House of Lords* (London, 1846).
MofP	*Return of the Names of Every Member Returned to Serve in Each Parliament* (London, 1759).
Nalson	John Nalson, *Impartial Collection of the Great affairs of State*, 2 vols. (London, 1682–83).
P.R.O.	Public Record Office, London.
Rushworth	John Rushworth, *Historical Collections of Private Passages of State*, 8 vols. (London, 1721).
Russell, *1621–1629*	Conrad Russell, *Parliaments and English Politics 1621–1629* (Oxford, 1979).
VCH Ches.	*Victoria County History: Cheshire.*
VCH Wilts.	*Victoria County History: Wiltshire.*

AN EXPLANATORY NOTE

THE editorial conventions used in this edition of Sir Thomas Aston's diary of the Short Parliament are described in detail below (pp.xv–xvi). Aston paginated his manuscript and his page numbers are indicated in the text by **bold type**. The cross-references in the footnotes and appendices refer, therefore, to these page numbers and not to the pagination of the modern edition.

I. INTRODUCTION

1. THE DIARY AND THE DIARIST

THE discovery of the diary of Sir Thomas Aston, a member for Cheshire, for the short Parliament of 1640 provides the richest available source for that assembly. A comparison of Aston's reporting of business in the lower house with the *Commons Journal* establishes that the baronet was an assiduous attender of debates in his first and only parliament. Aston recorded more speeches, and recorded speeches more thoroughly, than any other observer of its proceedings. Always careful to name the speakers whose contributions he noted, he preserved the speeches of 140 MPs, almost twice the number of speakers identified by other sources. It is here that many readers will find Aston's diary of greatest interest, as the richness of his reporting of debates puts flesh on the bones of many MPs who have previously been little more than names to historians. Thanks to Aston we can learn something of the content of parliamentary bills which have hitherto been known to us only by their titles, and discover what was controversial about them.[1] His thoroughness is exceptional by the standards of diaries not only for the Short Parliament but for all the parliaments of the first half of the seventeenth century. Even Sir Simonds D'Ewes' account of the Long Parliament is less comprehensive.

If its length is one chief merit of Aston's diary (it is nearly 47,000 words long), it also benefits from the straightforwardness of its reporting. Although a man of strong convictions, Sir Thomas did not allow them to colour his account which, unlike the parliamentary diaries of so many of his contemporaries, is unadorned by editorial judgements or asides. Despite—or because of—its objectivity, the diary brings alive, as no other source does, the mood of the Commons in the spring of 1640, and the deep sense of grievance and profound mistrust which, the document makes clear, was directed not only against the king's ministers but against Charles himself. Aston's aim is clear: to record what he heard. His motives, however, for producing such an objective account of the parliament remain tantalizingly obscure.

The diary is not without its weaknesses. Its record of formal addresses, such as those of the king and of the Lord Keeper, is sketchy, and Aston is often confused about the election disputes which arose

[1]See Appendix D. There is only one bill recorded in the *Commons Journal* which Aston fails to mention.

so frequently. Those deficiencies can be remedied, however, if we use the diary along side the other sources for the parliament. Indeed, it is in conjunction and comparison with those other sources that the diary becomes most useful. They are listed, day by day, in Appendix A, so that the reader can set Aston's account beside them. Here the work of Esther Cope, who in a volume in this series in 1977 brought together the diaries which were then known, is invaluable.

Aston's papers in the British Library and at Aston Lodge throw no light on his reasons for keeping a parliamentary diary. Born in 1600, he belonged to an ancient and notable Cheshire family which had settled near Runcorn many generations earlier. His father, John, was sewer to Queen Anne and married Maude, daughter of Robert Needham of Sherton, Shropshire. A number of his forefathers had been knighted, but it was Sir Thomas who raised the family to the status of major gentry in the shire. He was made baronet in 1628. Sir Thomas was educated at Macclesfield Grammar School, at Brasenose College, Oxford, and probably at Lincoln's Inn. His first marriage, in 1627, was to Magdalene, daughter of Sir John Poulteney of Leicestershire. None of their four children survived to adulthood, and Anne died in 1635, an event commemorated in a celebrated allegorical painting by John Souch.[1] By that year Sir Thomas was a gentleman of the privy chamber. His brother John was likewise a courtier.[2] Yet Sir Thomas skilfully combined his courtly connections with a resistance to the payment of ship money which secured his prominence in the county community and his victory, together with his partner Sir William Brereton, in the bitterly contested county election in the spring of 1640. In the civil war Aston would be an ardent royalist and episcopalian, Brereton a zealous parliamentarian and religious radical. In the spring of 1640, when the county's leaders were agreed in opposing royal policies, those divisions lay in the future. In November, when events had drawn the two men apart, Brereton defeated Aston in the election to the Long Parliament.[3]

[1]J. P. Earwaker, *East Cheshire* (2 vols., London, 1877), II, pp.10, 160, 317, 448–49; G. Ormerod, *History of Cheshire*, revised by G. Helsby (3 vols., London, 1882), I, pp.532–35; *DNB; VCH Ches.*, II, pp.42, 119; *AO;* Anthony Wood, *Athenae Oxonienses,* revised by Philip Bliss (5 vols., London, 1815), II, pp.184–85; *CSPD*, 1628–29, pp.222, 225. The painting is in the Manchester Art Gallery. C. H. Collins Baker, 'John Souch of Chester', *Connoisseur* (1928), pp.131–32. I am grateful to Mrs Dorothy Owen for this reference.

[2]I am grateful to Mr Peter Salt for bringing to my attention a warrant in the Lord Chamberlain's warrant books describing Aston as 'a Gentleman Extraordinary of the Privy Chamber' (P.R.O. LC5/134, p.170). John Aston (*d. 1650*) was active in royal service (e.g. *CSPD*, 1629–31, p.161) and his adventures in the Bishops' War are described in his journal published in 'North Country Diaries', *Surtees Society* (1910).

[3]For a discussion of Aston's role in the Cheshire ship money controversy, see Peter Lake, 'The Collection of Ship Money in Cheshire during the Sixteen-thirties: A Case

Despite that setback Sir Thomas emerged, between the meeting of
the Long Parliament and the outbreak of the civil war, as England's
leading lay defender of the Book of Common Prayer and of the
episcopal government of the Church of England.[1] In petitions, manuscripts and publications he pleaded for the 'Church of Elizabeth and
James', that is for the Church as it had been before the onset of
Laudian innovations and 'corruptions'.[2] By 1642 he had won a sig-
nificant portion of the Cheshire gentry to the royal cause. He fought
enthusiastically for the king, although with limited success. In
November 1645 he was wounded and captured in a bloody skirmish
near Bridgnorth. He died either there of his wounds or in captivity in
1646.[3]

II. EDITORIAL DECISIONS AND PRACTICES

A. *The Text.*   The manuscript diary of Sir Thomas Aston measures
$7\frac{1}{2}$ inches by 6 inches and contains 220 pages. It covers the entire
parliament from 13 April to 5 May 1640, and includes fourteen pages
of committee reports as an appendix. It is bound in limp vellum with
parchment thongs. Occasional pages appear to have been inserted at
a later date. The manuscript is in Aston's hand, and though in places
it is difficult to decipher, it is almost certainly a fair copy made from
notes.[4] Aston may have known a form of shorthand, so full is his record

---

Study of Relations Between Central and Local Government', *Northern History* (1981),
passim; Elaine Marcotte, 'Shrieval Administration of Ship Money in Cheshire, 1637:
Limitations of Early Stuart Governance', *Bulletin of the John Rylands University Library
of Manchester* (1975), pp.148–50; John Morrill, *Revolt of the Provinces* (London, 1976,
1980), p.25. For further reading about the spring elections of 1640 in Cheshire, see
CSPD, 1639–40, pp.564–65, 590–91; *VCH Ches.*, II, p.108; John Morrill, *Cheshire 1630–
1660* (London, 1974), pp.25, 33; Lake, 'Collection', pp.67–68; John Morrill, 'Sir
William Brereton and England's Wars of Religion', *Journal of British Studies* (1985). I
am grateful to Dr Morrill for showing me a typescript of his article before publication.
[1]Morrill, *Cheshire*, pp.37, 45–56; Morrill, *Provinces*, pp.48–49, 150–52; Anthony Fletcher, *The Outbreak of the English Civil War* (London, 1981), pp.91–124, 283–91, *passim*;
Judith Maltby, 'Approaches to the Popular Support for the Book of Common Prayer
and the Established Church in late Elizabethan and Early Stuart England' (Cambridge
Ph.D thesis in progress).
[2]Sir Thomas Aston's published works on this subject are: *A Remonstrance Against
Presbytery* (n.p., 1641); *A Collection of Sundry Petitions* (n.p., 1642).
[3]Morrill, *Cheshire*, pp.53–54, 56, 64–65, 75–76; Ronald Hutton, *The Royalist War Effort
1642–1646* (London, 1982), pp.7–8, 22–30, 39, 44–46, 97–98, 127, 192–93; R. N. Dore,
The Civil Wars in Cheshire (Chester, 1966), *passim*; H.M.C., 13th Report, Portland Mss.
1, p.306; B. L. Thomason Tracts E.309(24). The owner of the diary, Mr Howard
Talbot, is planning a biography of Sir Thomas which will deal in depth with his
military career.
[4]There are occasional marginal notes in the text, such as 'Lib:A', which may refer to
the original rough notes.

of debate. There is no evidence to indicate how long after the events described the fair copy was made (Aston did not die until 1646).

B. *Editorial Conventions.*

1. *Abbreviations.* Generally abbreviations have been extended. Where there is room for reasonable doubt, the extension appears in italic surrounded by square brackets. Modern pound signs have been used. Precedents cited (e.g. '6 H. 8') are not extended and appear as in the manuscript. Etc., &, are retained as in the manuscript.

2. *Spelling.* Original spelling is retained except in the case of 'two' which frequently appears as 'tow' in the manuscript.

3. *Punctuation.* Extensive liberties are taken with Aston's very inconsistent punctuation. The diary consists largely of incomplete sentences. His use of strokes to divide up phrases has not been retained. The advice of the editors of the Yale *Commons Debates 1628* is applicable here: 'Readers should feel free to try their hand at revising the punctuation in any part of the text that in their view makes unsatisfactory sense as it stands, or might make different but equal sense if punctuated in a different way'.[1]

4. *Capitals.* Capitals have been added at the beginning of sentences created by the editing of the original punctuation. However, capitals are retained when Aston has clearly used them. In addition, double 'ff's have been changed to capital 'F's.

5. *Marginal Notes.* The few marginal notes in the text appear in the footnotes. Aston made heavy, but unhelpful, use of brackets in the margins beside the remarks of many MPs. Their purpose is not clear and they have not been retained.

6. *Editorial Insertions.* The editor has occasionally made insertions into the text to aid the reader's comprehension of the syntax or to provide information. These words are in square brackets.

7. *Quotation Marks.* Quotation marks have been occasionally added in the text to aid the reader.

8. *Pagination and Notes to References within the Text.* Aston paginated, not foliated, his diary. His pagination is indicated in the text in bold type.

---

[1] *C.D. 1628*, I, p.48.

II. THE SHORT PARLIAMENT (1640)
DIARY OF SIR THOMAS ASTON

[Monday, 13 April]

p.1 The proceedings of the house of parlament the 13th April 1640. The first Ceremony is the riding to the Abbey.[1] The King & Lords in state [in the House of Lords]. Then the Kings speech[2] recommends a Speaker.[3] Then the house of Commons & offer the Speaker [Sir John Glanville] the chayre whoe makes many delays & excuses & at last takes it. Then the house is adiourned till the 15:th of April. The oaths of Supremacy & alleageance adminnistered by the Earle Marshall to as many as were present. Then a Commission to Some of them to sweere the rest, which all men must take ere they sitt in the house.

[Wednesday, 15 April]

The 15th. The 15th at two a Clock: all meete & attended the Speaker to the paynted chamber wheere hee makes a short Speech, praying the King to[4] recommend a more able man etc. Which the King answeares by his Keeper & approoves his ability. Then hee accepts & makes a speech.[5] Wheerin hee had many very good thinges. Monarchy Royall is of all sorts of Government, the most excellent. Which in this Common wealth I hope none denyes, if any such I wish Confusion to them. England is your seate of right. Scotland your byrth place. God make them sensible. Ireland imitates England by a quick progresse. **p.2** France must be your attendant. Then put your king in mynd, of his gratious expression in print. That the Liberty of the people strengthens the kings prerogative, & the kings prerogative preserves the people. That the king is free from iniustice, the ministers lyable being by theyr oaths bound to doe iustice, & having noe excuse but a voyd Command. His majesties great grace & Iustice had bin manifested in his assent to the petition of right. The woords of assent repeated which may rise up in iudgment against all that censure it to all ages. His mercy appeered in not drawing his sword of iustice

---

[1]Marginal note: 'Lib. A:'. Bishop Matthew Wren of Ely preached.

[2]The king's speech, delivered largely by the Lord Keeper, was chiefly concerned to show that the war with Scotland was the main cause for the calling of the parliament.

[3]Marginal note: 'Lib. A:'.

[4]Marginal note: 'vid. Lib. A. i'.

[5]Marginal note: 'vid. Speech at Large in Quires'.

against the subiects of Scotland: His Rule being, *posse et nolle Nobile*. Without love in unity hee that Commands in love hath onely power to command both the purse to pay & the hands to fight. *Inseperabiles, Insuperabiles*. Then humbly moves for the Commons that they may be free in theyr persons from arrests & troubles to goe about his Majesties service. That they may have freedome of Speech. That they may have accesse to his majestie. That his majestie wilbe pleased to Construe all things to the best.

p.3 The Lord Keeper [John, Lord Finch of Fordwich].
That the King was pleased with his humblenes in accepting as well as with his modesty in refuzing. That his first enemy had crept into mens breasts expectation, but iealousie was too base to be entertayned. Then reflects on the Considerations of the Kingdome, in the Frame a Monarchy, in the Nature hereditary. On the King: not to be paraleld for mercy. That in 15 yeares scarce any man felt the axe but in petty Causes. Then pronounces an anathema to all that alter Government which was buylt on 5 pyllars.
1. Religion which Seazons all other virtues. To the reverend prelates & theyr predecessors wee owe the preservation of our Religion. That wee had Gates of Saphire onix & pretious stones aswell as gould & silver etc.[1] God forbid God should be served as ploughmen.
2. Iudges not exceeded in any age: if not iust noe reazon to be excused: they have both the example of Iustice in the King & strict chardge from him.
3. The great Lords, never soe great in Number, Courage greater.
4. Commerce which is our Royall Myne our Indies.
5. Our happy union. *Si colledimur frangimur*. Then encouragement to proceed, the King well approves nothing takes a good nature soe much as humblenes & freedome. Grants our petitions. &c:
Then wee Returne to the house.[2] And the Keeper [*sic*] reads an act for Conforming apparell. Then is requyred (though not usuall) to report the Kings speech the next morning.

[Thursday, 16 April]

p.4 The 16th April. First prayer in the morning. The speaker reades a set prayer. 2d: an act read for Recoveryes by infants under 21 by vouchers to be voyd. To preiudice none in reversion unlesse partyes. 3d: fall to chooze the committee of priveledges of elections in which

---

[1]Possibly an allusion to Ezekiel 28:13.

[2]Aston does not record that the King spoke to accept Glanville as speaker and to remind him of his duties: 'That you giving Me your timely Help in this great Affair, I shall give a willing Ear to all your just Grievances' (*L.J.*, IV, p.54).

much Confusion. Every man calling on whom hee affects & all at once. Soe those next the chayre name most of the Committee. Then divers whoe were chozen for severall places. Release which they please & take to another. Then a dispute whether any Mayors could be of the house which was very doubtfull, presidents vouched both wayes. Mayor of Cambridge, mayor of Newport out, not to be returned.

Sir peeter Ruddle.
That he knew 2 mayors of NewCastle sate & served. Three of 4 returned for one place not to sit till it be determined order. Noe man to name any man but the speaker.

Mr. secretary.
Brings a Command from the King about the letter, sent by the Scotts to the French king.[1] Informes that hee had bin sent with the Lord Cottington [Francis, Lord Cottington] & Mr. Atturney [Sir John Bankes, Attorney General] to the Lord Lowdun [John Campbell, Lord Loudon] to examyne him & he confessed his hand, but pretended he did not understand French, & thought it had bin onely to pray him to mediate with the king. Lesleyes hand I knew: And prayes a speedy dispatch.

Mr. Grymston.
That it was Convenient to Consider the danger but that this distance was far off, he wished it further. Wee had danger at Home as Considerable.[2] That wee ought to deale with the Body politick as body naturall. First cleanse the blood then all scabbs &c will fall off, if the danger as great cause to Consider at Home. The great charter granted by King Iohn, Confirmed 37 times. By the kings graunt in the petition of right. Had not some contrary to Iustice, religion & conscience out of parlament over ruled acts of parlament. Then shewed us the effects. 2 things enquyrable. 1st what done Contrary to our liberty and 2ly whoe have done it. Then recyted Artaxerxes woords: **p.5** whoe have not done the will of God & the lawe, let iudgment be done upon them.[3] What can wee hope for more then wee have had, wee had the Royall woord of our master. Wee cannot Complaine of want of good lawes, but of those that have obstructed the passage of them. Let them be made examples.

Sir Beniamin Ruddyar.
That wee have a great dore opened to do good. The kings heart

---

[1]The King discussed this letter in his speech at the opening of the parliament on 13 April. See Cope, pp.58, 96, 122, 233, 244.
[2]Marginal note: 'vid. at large, Lib: A: 3'.
[3]Ezra 7:26.

appeares in calling us together. Parlaments have bin soe unhappy that the name of a parlament hath bin had in Reproach. It lyes in us to restore parlaments. Wee know whence the breach of the first parlament came that ere was broke in England. Remissnes in religion a cause. Papists have stood in Competition with us whoe have bin the best subiects & carryed it. I approve theyr emulation not arrogance. Light expells darknes without noyse, animosity & fiercenesse becomes noe religion. Let us tenderly dresse the wounds of the Common wealth. The Splinters of a broken parlament give the greatest wounds to the body politique & had need to be drawne out with a tender hand. In the 14th of E.3. great Sums weare granted to a warr in France. In the 15th he sumoned a parlament wheerin they were full of Iealousies which soone ended in discontent. In the 17th he cald another to make atonement, which tooke successe never differed. A parlament is the bed of reconciliation betweene a king & his people. Let us not fall with too much vehemence on our owne greivances, before wee looke on the kings occasions. Equanimity is the best temper. All kings as naturally love power as people liberty. Sometimes examples are more necessary then lawes. But at this time unseazonable. Tis fit to reconsyle the kings grace with those. The power of necessity & power of a King will not be long in one hand. I could never heare that poore narrowe woord of proiecting applyed to the King without indignation. Let us be partrons of a parlament now wee have it, what would not wee have given for a parlament within these fewe moneths. Let us not dote more on a Imaginary parlament then a reall. As long as wee have parlaments, wee shall fund our selves. When they are gone wee are lost.[1]

Sir Francis Seymar.[2]
Wee are as loving subiects as ever any; & as ready to supply. The time onely Considerable. If wee soe serve him as to forgett our selves wee should doe him disservice. If wee speake our grievances it is the greatest greivance of which wee can speake.[3] **p.6** His majesties care & love may be seene in hearing our greivances. How have wee bin wrongd in freedome of speech, iudgments against the members of the house, not soe considerable in the parlticulares as in the generalls; against reazon, conscience, Iustice. Iudges questioned in parlament for acts done out of parlament, I have knowne, but of acts in parlament censured by Iudges, tis newe. For my part I had rather suffer for speaking truth, then truth should suffer for want of speaking. I know

---

[1]See Cope, pp.250–51.
[2]Aston places this speech on 16 April, which strengthens Professor Cope's case for placing it on that day. See Cope, p.298.
[3]Marginal note: '(Lib: A: 4)'.

not why these should reflect upon the King. The sun is alwayes cleare though sometimes thick clouds or mists betwixt us & it, but what avayles it us unlesse they be cleared up. Let the fountayne be never soe cleare if it run through muddy channells what can be expected wee must cleanse them. Religion is out faced by papists. NonResidents get livings, & set payed hyrelings over the flock. These the scripture calls dumb doggs.[1] Others preach themselves not the Gospell, tell Kings of an unlimited power. People noe propertye in theyr goods. In the 2d. place are the violences of our libertyes, which have bin confirmed by a king. God forbid any of them should be broke. He is a traitor that shall betray a king to his enemies, is noe lesse that shall betray him to him selfe. It can never be other wayes when acts of power shalbe above lawes, & lawes shalbe over ruled by iudgment against lawes & Libertyes.

Sir John Culpepper.
2 things to enquyred. First whether the house be setled. 2d: to begin with other things but a *Jove principium*.

Sir Henry mildmay.
Mooving against having applauzes, & discountenancing others.

Sir Henry vane
Moves to settle the Committees.

Mr. pymm.[2]
To settle the Committees, & that things evident of proofe & not doubtfull should be mooved in the house.

Committees.
The Committee for elections to sit Tuesday, Thursday, & Saturday.[3] Mr. Iones in the chayre Religion Mundayes.[4] Mr. Crew for Greivances wednesdays.[5] Mr. Glyn, for Courts of Iustice frydayes.[6] Mr. peard in the chayre these of the whole house.

---

[1] Isaiah 56:10.
[2] See below, **pp.198–200**.
[3] I.e. the committee of Privileges, of which Aston was a member. *C.J.*, II, p.4.
[4] A committee of the whole house. *C.J.*, II, p.3. Probably Charles Jones.
[5] A committee of the whole house. *C.J.*, II, p.3.
[6] A committee of the whole house. *C.J.*, II, p.4.

[Friday, 17 April]

p.7 The 17th of April.

The Speaker

Makes Report of the kings speech & the Keepers, In which he tooke the liberty to have helpe of notes. In the first part he treated of the nature of parlaments. That they were the auntient, great generall Councell of the kingdome, wheerin wee were invited participate of the Graces of the king. The king was Confident of our affections. That he sequestred the memory of all former discouragements. That the end was necessary, our common preservation. The Higher Councells were lodg'd in the arke of his bozom, & it was a presumption for any Uzza to touch the arke.[1] He had layd aside the Beames of his majestie not put them of, nor guyding of the chariott, wee may approach to it. That the King alone kept us from forreigne dangers. Our honor safe compar'd to Gideons fleece,[2] our fleece was dry when it raigned blood in all other places, but what was this. *Si foris hostem non inueni domi inueni*. The king claymes his entry by blood not by bloodshed. That towards Scotland he had used all indulgences. *Civiles furores peperit nimia felicitas*, the grounds shewed. Some men of Beliall[3] had blowne the trumpet. Theere were shebas insolent & rebellious, to the defection of his majestie & his Crowne. Lead a multitude into disloyalty & rebellious treazon. Taken up Armes against the king & by some Achitophells[4] Counsell seized Trophees of Royalty & assumd Royall power. The king in his gratious nature *cum nec vincere, nec vinci sine periculo posse.* **p.8** Upon promises of future loyalty returnes the Army. That they onely prevaricate to gett time since his returne they have treated with forreigne states, under the hands of Ring leaders. England was observed to be of too tough a Complexion to be assayled at the fore doore, they must come in behynd. It had but two back doores. Ireland was one, & was Civiliz'd & from chardge become an ayd. Scotland was the other. In a weake body the ill humors have a flux to the sick place. Next he shewed us his majesties set resolution to have a powrefull army to reduce them, necessity that it should be soe. The chardge more then probably expected in his majesties coffers, which hee had not wasted in any vayne expence, this similed [*sic*] by a vapour drawne up & showred downe agayne. Tells us that his designe was cheifly for Scotland. He offered to us to participate in this great woorke. Counsells for proffitt admitt debate, Counsells for

---

[1] II Samuel 6:6–7; I Chronicles 13:9–10.
[2] Judges 6:38.
[3] See e.g., Deuteronomy 13:13; I Samuel 2:12; 10:27; 25:17; II Chronicles 13:17; II Corinthians 6:15.
[4] II Samuel 16:20–23.

safety requyre present redresse, the bleeding evill requyred such supply. Things that were the desires of the king. To lay aside other debates, and passe an act for soe many subsedies as this ayd requyres. The Session not to determine by his assent to that Bill. Adds that his majestie would not have proposed it but for straightnes of time, that he had secured £300000 for preserve [of] Barwick & Carlile. This would be of noe use without further supply till more graunted. There content to stay till releefe of greivances. That hee hold Tonnadge & Pondage by president as his Auncestors till graunted. **p.9** That he desire to clayme it by graunt of parlament. And would have a Bill prepared & penned with woords from the death of his father till this time. That Complying in these particulars, his woord was engaged to heare & releeve all towards winter. In reformation the king to goe with us. The king made the conclusion & produced the French letter.[1] Observations made on the stile *Au Roy*: a stile to the King of his subiects.

Mr. pymm
Tooke notice that this report had bin made by the kings speciall command, & desires it may be entered to be soe, & not made a president because the Speaker heares but with theyr eares as a servant, & but in extraordinary occasion ought not: observ'd that it came but by interception, that the French king did never receive much lesse entertaine the motion.

Mr. Controwler.
That the king will not impose without occasion.

Mr. Rowse.
Held greivances fitt to be spoke of. The Roote left untouch'd. That there was encdeavour to make union betwixt us & Roome. Sancta clara interpreted all the articles established by the house contrary to the sense of the house.[2] The woord puritan will serve against an arminian in the mouth of a papist against a papist in the mouth of a protestant &c. And I thinke in time will make us asham'd of our religion. Such ministers as refuzed to read the direction for morris dancers,[3] wheare a clearke would serve, are excommunicated & drive[n from] the kingdome; wee are Imposed monopolies & ship money &c.

---

[1] Lord Louden's letter. See above, **p.4**.
[2] Christopher Davenport, chaplain to Queen Henrietta Maria, was better known as Franciscus a Sancta Clara. *DNB*; Cope, p.146n. 12.
[3] *The King's Majesties Declaration to his Subjects Concerning Lawful Sports* (1633).

p.10 Mr. pymm.[1]

Hee that takes away weights does as good service as whoe adds wings. In the beginning god made the world by Modell. He offers a Modell under 3 Heads. 1st: against liberty of parlaments; it was a caution *ne ledas mentem.* That governes all the rest. Priveledges of parlament are of great consequence. The greatest perrogative of the King that he can doe noe wrong. Our priveledge was broke, the keeper commanded not to put to the question, the house not to speake. The speaker is the servant of the house. Many Members Imprizoned. Sentences in inferior Courts past against them for things done in parlament. Lye in prizon under pretence of no baling. Our meeting heere as a representative body is our life, when wee are parted wee fall in peices, this is the greatest greivance. Greivances against religion; connivence of the Romish. Those concurrent with noe religion, they admitt noe superiority. They are in themselves quyet for a time but by the pope are carryed about as in the *primum mobile.*

In religion:

1st: a suspension made of the lawes & a proffitt made of them.

2d: that they are admited to Counsells.

3d: that they have places in the Common wealth, have reputation of a Nuncio. It hath ever bin the study of Roome to devize means to reduce England.

4. Innovations, to make us more easy to be translated that wee by little & little digest popery. Divers bookes, disputes in universities, preaching & mayntaning popish poynts.

5. Inducing popish Ceremonies, bowing to altars & pictures that when wee have put the flesh the dry bones may be inanimated[2] **p.11**

6. discouragements on the professors, whoe should be gently dealt withall.

7. Many urged to things for which wee have noe ground at all, as punishing those that will not read the bookes of may Games, & sportings on the Sabbath day for which they have noe publique command by the king.

2[d]. 1. The encroachment of authority by Eclesiasticall Courts to fyne & Imprizon.

2. They disclayme Iurisdiction from kings they will have it from heaven.

3. That ordinaryes get out articles to examyne without the Lawe.

3d. Greivances against the Civill government. 1st Tonnadge & poundage without authority, auntient Customes due by prescription

---

[1] Pym's famous speech about grievances reportedly took two hours to deliver. See Professor Cope's discussion of the different versions of the text (pp.299–302).

[2] Ezekiel 37.

acknowledged. Those have bin enlarged but never any imposition layd but by parlament. There was in Q. E1: time an imposition layd on currenz.[1] 3 Iudges then call'd to consult & they differed in opinions. Greivance in excesse, that the chardge exceeds the commodity. Greivance in the clayme & imployment not for the use of the seas but as rizing out of the prerogative.

4. The Greivance of Knighthood. Not alone that it was applyed to men Capable of it, but it went to Tertennants to Coppy holders to merchants. It was aggravated in that they pleaded & could not be heard, but were put in issues which run on not till they fyned with the Court whence they issued but with the Commissioners.

5. A greivance, that there are monopolies upon things growing & consumed in the Kingdomes.

p.12 6. The 6th is Shipmoney, a iudgment agaisnt all lawe bookes noe president, noe man scapes it nor limitts of it.[2]

7. The Forrest busines, extending it beyond all bounds that taken of by act of parlament. The iudges are to answeare it.

8. A farming of publique Nusances which are at first found Nusances but when Compounded noe Nusance amongst these that of depopulation.

9. The military chardges by letters from the Lords, or king, pressing of men, munition, horses, & such like by Lord Lieutenants of theyr owne heads.

10. Extra Iudiciall Cases by iudges, when noe cause in tryall, in Legall iudgments wee have remedyes by writts of error, against these nowe.

11. That the authority of Courts of Iustice, starchamber establishes nuizances, that, that [sic] which was ordayned to punish greivances should be made a Court of revenue. I am High now but must goe Higher yet.

12. The Lords of the Councell whoe had theyr originall from this house, had an oath administered to doe iustice. If a greivance that Iustices & inferior persons have theyr hands in such busines. What if those Lords & that board frame & Countenance Monopolies as beneath they dignity: I must yet goe Higher to the king himselfe.

13. As the King hath a transcendent power, that this High power should be soe used, [that] Monopolies should be set out under the power of proclamations.

14. Yet I must goe above all these. Which is the truth of God, the Bond of conscience: Bookes writt sermons preached, to give an unlimited power to the king, to take away peoples libertyes. **p.13** Such tenants had bin thought fitt to be sentenc'd & punished by this house. Manwaring for this doctrine was brought very lowe, hee never sawe

---

[1] Aston is thinking of Bate's Case of 1606.
[2] Hampden's Case.

man in all his life lower, soe lowe that hee thought hee should not have seene him soe soone stept up into a Bishoprick. Tis well if his preferment does not encourage others.[1]

15. A Cause of all these greivances is the intermission of parlaments; the King may call when hee will but the Lawe requyres once a yeare.[2] The King receives noe benefit by these. They are more preiudiciall to the king then subiects.

1st. The Breach of liberty cutts of the Communion of subiects with the king.

2. Deprives the people, of his most substantiall support which is a Supply of parlaments, which can never be sould chardged nor incumbred.

3. Losse of Reputation abroad, when hee had all theyr purses at command, ellse the palatinate had not bin lost. The king of England might have seeized upon the Indies.

4. By the greivances of religion hee hath not the support for a party to abroad. Hee hath lost hearts at Home.

5. The Industry & valour of the nation is diminished by it. Men are discouraged & disheartned in theyr wayes.

6. It makes way for ill men to ingratiate themselves in the kings service. He that can be an instrument in these designes it salves all blemishes.

7. It breads Iealouzies on both sides, it makes way to distempers. Such as one sommers profitt consumes more then all these bring in.

Heere he recollected one thing formerly forgott. That was Imposition upon such things as never came into England. A merchant[3] in Fraunce trading into Spayne &c. shall have an imposition on that he never brings heere. **p.14** That these illegall things come not to the kings Coffers in a legall way, are a great part to the damage of the subiect goes to the officers. Instances in the new imposition on wynes wheerin the king receives but £30000 a yeare, the Farmers get £80000 the retaylers £232000[4] a yeare & the subiect suffers all this. For the Remedies he shall offer them to the Consideration of the house to be determined & then to goe to the Lords.

Sir Gilbert pickering of Northamptonshire presents a petition of greivances against shipmoney & innovation in matters of religion, delivered him at his election in Northamptonshire.

[1]Roger Mainwaring was made bishop of St. David's in 1636. See Russell, *1621–1629*, pp.375, 396, 400, 404.

[2]4 Edward III c.14; 36 Edward III c.10 (Cope p.155, n.1).

[3]An English merchant. See Cope, pp.156, 219, 259–60.

[4]Aston had a French wine importing business in Chester. Peter Lake, 'The Collection of Ship Money in Cheshire during the Sixteen-thirties: A Case Study of Relations Between Central and Local Government', *Northern History* (1981), pp. 46–47.

Mr. Ball.
That petitions ought first to be presented to the Committee.

Sir walter Earle.
That petitions presented at the doore may be shewed, but by members of the house ought to be read.

Sir Gilbert Gerrard.
Presents another petition from his county.

Sir Nathaniel Barneston.
Presents another from Suffolke.

Mr. Kerton.
Moves that mr. pym may prepare the remedies that wee may goe to the Lords soe to the king soe to the kings affayres.

Sir John Hotham.
That they may be prepared to morrowe.

Mr. Rigby.
That least misinterpretation be made to the king, soe great a revenewe being to fall from his Coffers, that it may be reported withall. That these may be supplyed by a Constant revenue to be setled by us, for the preservation of his Crowne & defence.

For the better dispatch of affayres ordered to sitt all day if need be.

[Saturday, 18 April]

p.15 April the 18th.
Sir Harbottle Grimston, Essex.
A petition from the freeholders of Essex: against innovations in religion, vayne alterations in Churches, to the increase of heresies, monopolies.[1] Motion that they must affirme on theyr creditts. The petition delivered by the Countrey.

Sir william Litton. Hartford.
Another petition against innovations in religion.[2] Contrary to Canons, Rubrick & booke of prayers. Denying Sacraments to 100 in a Congregation a whole yeare: more collected then ship money, or fifteenes.

[1] The petition also mentioned ship money, forest fines and impositions. For the text, see Cope, pp.275–76.
[2] For the text, see Cope, pp.277–78.

Against Feodaryes, monopolies. Lastly shipmoney & that parlaments once a yeare.

Alderman Atkins. Norwich.
Petition directed to the Governors of the Citty.[1] Innovations in religion, erecting the altars, none to receive without kneeling at the rayles: monopolies on soape, Coales. Shipmoney 2ˢ per pound on howses to the ministers of the Citty. A parlament yearly.

Mr. Hyde.
A greivance unmentioned. My Lord Marshalls Court a Court of honor.[2] A Court in one night to growe up to that height by the stile a man would looke for some glorious advantage to the Common wealth. If I owe my taylour money I can pay hime in his owne Bills, quitt him with his owne ill manners. Twas a unservable condition of him that calld a swan a goose to lye in prizon for it. An appendant to this is the pageantry of it the Heralds: other greivances are at an end when wee dye, these afflict our carcasses. Gentlemen how ever they live yet questionles [that] they might dye as cheape as other men; which they may not it must cost them £5 more. A gentleman a lawyer sent for to acknowledge under his hand, that it was lawe, because he had delivered his opinion that he knew noe lawe for it.

p.16 Mr. Knightley.
A petition from Northampton to the effect of the Former.[3]

Mr. Secretary.
Upon the Committee for the fast report, nothing to be sent in writing as not with the dignity of the house but to be left to theyr woords to that sense.[4]

A generall fast. The speaker avoyds the mace remooved. Mr. Grymston called to the chayre.

Sir Iohn Strangewayes.
To the Liberty of Speech, to give life to this body. Treason or felony to be tryed against any member of the house. But misdeameanors of

[1]'The Humble Petition of the Maior; Sheriffes, Aldermen and Citizens of the Citty of Norwich' in Cope. For the text, see Cope, p.279. John T. Evans, *Seventeenth Century Norwich* (Oxford, 1979), p.95.

[2]Hyde becamethe chairman of a committee to investigate the Earl Marshal's Court in the Long Parliament. D'Ewes (Notestein), pp.375, 375n.3.

[3]Sir Gilbert Pickering (Northamptonshire) presented a petition on 17 April (see above, **p.14**). For the text see Cope, p.275.

[4]It was ordered that a message concerning a fast should be sent to the Lords, but that it should be deferred until Monday (20 April). *C.J.*, II, p.6.

the house, not to be questioned out of the house. Things last day to be questioned, the I [first] day of next parlament. Query that Sir Iohn Eliot &c wickedly intending to lay a scandal. Query & uniust aspersion upon the Counsell, query this in starchamber. Priveldge pleaded. Refered to iudges. 7 maynt, 5 against it. This was by *habeas Corpus* to Kings Bench. Plead same priveldg upon *nihill dicit* fynds them Guylty & fine them prayes ayd from long Roabe. The Kings soune the great Duke of Lancaster questioned. The Duke of Saffol [*sic*] H 6 time, questioned heere. King Iames time verulam[1] & Duke [of] Buckingham.[2] 2. Whether wee have power to give or not to give. If the King when, wheere & as oft as he will, wee are all tennants at will. The iudges give King warrant preached & printed, that without parlament he may impose. **p.17** That if wee refuze wee incur damnation. The King gave way to Dispute: a iudgment without lawe, without president, without Custome; that these 2: liberty of Speech & the ship money setled, in the poynt of property. Then to manifest our duty to the best of Kinges. This Generally approoved.

Sir Ralph Hopton.
Religion more materiall. Not all now to be disputed but some i [*sic*] wherin ordinaryes be impose on mens Consciences, or purses without lawes.

Mr. Hambden.
Not two many thinges at once. Least wee looze our end: begin with the first liberty of Speaking: to send to the Lordes to meete in the afternoone.

Mr. Iones.[3]
Present at all proceedings in star chamber & King's Bench. Starchamber disclaymed it. They pleaded to the Iurisdiction: That the iudgment was that they had treapas'd against the peace, & were iudgd upon defalt.

Mr. pymm.
That this day was set a part for the generalles without limitations.

---

[1]Sir Francis Bacon.
[2]The cases of Bacon and Buckingham are discussed by Colin G.C. Tite, *Impeachment and Parliamentary Judicature in Early Stuart England* (London, 1974), pp.110–18, 178–217; for the case of the duke of Suffolk, see B.P. Wolfe, *Henry VI* (London, 1981), pp.221–29; R.A. Griffiths, *The Reign of Henry VI* (London, 1981), pp.674–84. I am grateful to Dr Rosemary Horrox for these references.
[3]Probably Charles Jones: see Cope, p.159, n.7.

Lord of falkland.
That first liberty of Speech, elles how shall wee speake of the greatest
or least.

Mr. Frauncis Seymor.
The 2d as necessary, elles whyles wee are heere our goodes are taken
in the Countrey.

p.18 Mr. pymm.
That it may be put to question. Whether the inhibiting of speaking
& the Speaker be a greivance against the liberty of the house.

Question resolved all 'I'.

Mr. Glynn.
That the starchamber did overrule it, had noe priveledge. That the
iudgment in Kinges Bench, hath bin approoved as a iudgment, which
till wee see the Record wee cannot iustly adiudge being a Court of
Record.

Sir Robert Harlowe
Let us not begin with the feete but with the head. With the chayre
the offences done by the speaker the last day[1] in refuzing the question.

Mr. Kirton.
The iudgment cleere, not to give that respect to an inferior Court.

Mr. waller.
To know our libertyes, elles wee shall never lymm [*sic*] to the life
without the substance.[2] Desir'd the woordes.

Mr. pymm.
If wee may not speake, nor put question wee doe nothing: the last
speaker avowed a command not to put to question.

Mr. Treasurer.
Upon the president. Noe man but sensible one at that unhappy
dissolution. Wee render our Kings of theyr priveledges, if in Courts
of Iustice not without Recordes. **p.19** Wee desire the end why should
wee touch that which may not be soe well relish'd.

---

[1]A reference to the 'tumult' on the last day of the parliament of 1628–29. The
following debate is a discussion of that event. See Russell, *1621–1629*, pp.415–16.

[2]The image is of an artist's model. I am grateful to Professor Conrad Russell for
throwing light on this phrase.

Mr. vaughan.

2 things that stick. The priveledges broke. How.

1. Fact: the speaker would put noe question, the house silenced.

2. Courts in Iustice that not without Record.

The first in mens memories.

Sergeant Wyld.

A wittnes in last parlament. A protestation tendred: a message to attend the upper house: one tore the paper. Though lost: the matter remembered, mooved to be put to the question. Speaker sayd he had received a Command to the Contrary. Query if the act of the speaker himselfe. If an act of Higher power a breach to the priveledge.

Mr. Hyde.

Whether it be breach, then whether done.

Mr. Harbert.

That wee were out of the way. First to the question which shall have priority.

Mr. Iones.

Though the parlament assembled by the Kings authority yet expressly not to be dissolved upon pretence of a message from the king without consent of the house.

Mr. Grymston.

That he had noe voyce but yet was not in opinion secluded.

Mr. Hamden.

Mooved to order to send for the Records in starchamber or Kings Bench.

Mr. pymm.

Whether it bee reported as the opinion of the Committee that the Records be sent for. **p.20** The Committee noe authority to send a Mace till the house satt for the speaker to take his chayre then ordered which was ordered to be sent for presently.

Mr. Lewkener.

Present at the dissolution, the woords in his notes.[1] The house foreseeing something that might be displeazing, Hee [the Speaker] express'd that the house was adiourn'd. Hee was commanded to keepe the chayre. Hee pretended the kings service, desired not to be ruin'd for the Kings service. 'I leave not the chayre to disobey you but to

---

[1] Lewknor represented Midhurst in the parliament of 1628–29, and took notes of the proceedings as well as writing reports to the earl of Northampton. Keeler, p.252.

obey his majestie'. Obiected hee was the houses servant. I will not say I will not, but I will say I dare not put the question.

Mr. Controwler.
The black Rod was at the doore. *Cuius est Constituere eius est dissolvere.* If soe & the doore shut against him, then it was all one as if hee had adiourned.

Sir Hugh Chalmley.
Query to reforme our libertyes, not question what past. Hee would have the case determined by suppositions, if the speaker did deny to put the question, & if the members were forbid to speake, & if the house were adiourned without authority.

p.21 Mr. Harbert.
Would have us proceed upon the fact & upon greivances not upon suppositions.

Sir walter Earle.
Shall the speakers affirmation be taken by us to be the kings Command. The black Rod was but sent to summon us to come up to the Lords to heare dissolution theere.

Mr. Kerton.
That it was not usuall, the speaker brought messages from the King.

Sir Henry Vane.
That Sir Robert phillips[1] did frequently bring messages.

Mr. waller.
That the black Rod was not at the Doore. That he found the speaker denying the question.

Sir miles Fletwood.
The speaker[2] sayd I have a Command to adiourne the Court. Hee knowes speaker has delivered messages. Not to question the kings Command.

Sir peeter Hammon.[3]
Found Lords house distempered, found mr. speaker in the chayre, saying I am command[*ed*] to adiourne the house.
2. It was his majesties pleazure they should not speake: hee was desirous to keepe in the chayre. Hee refuz'd to put questions, was

---

[1] Sir Edward Phelips, Speaker 1604–1610.
[2] Sir Edward Phelips (Cope, p161n.3).
[3] For Heyman's behaviour at 'the tumult' which marked the end of the parliament of 1628–29, see Russell, *1621–1629*, pp.415–16.

Committed: prepared a lettre of Atturney to sue a *Habeas Corpus*: 13 weekes prizoner. Sent for, then tampered to petition, which he thought not with the liberty of the subiect: stayed till hee was punish't enought for his offence. After liberty to take the ayre.

p.22 Mr. Pymm.
Not to leave this question disputable: The act of adiourning the house ever the house has bin soe wary as to adiourne the house.

Mr. Controwler.
Necessary to see the Recordes. Before a question.

Mr. Ball.
Variety in the relations. Theerfore a subcommittee to Consider of what hath bin done to present it.

Mr. glyn.
2ds it. Mr. Controwler like wise.

Mr. pym.
That a Sub Committee cannot be made without the Consent of the whole house. The Committee appoynted.

Sir Hugh Cholmondlegh.
Would not have us depart ere wee lay a Brand upon ship money.

Mr. Herbert.
All respect to those that speake for the liberty & property of our goods. Yet those that speake not with moderation reserve not the respect usually given to this house. If wee upon soe deliberate a iudgment, whoe are sworne to mayntaine a iust prerogative shall upon a minute say wee shall lay a Brand upon soe great a iudgment least the King receive preiudice of us that proceed soe suddenly. If the King may by his right in defence of the Kingdome take it. We are too quick to stop the proceedings before iudgment.

p.23 Sir Hugh Cholmondleigh.
That if wee did not lay a Brand ere wee return'd home wee were too blame.

Mr. St. Iohn Answers Mr. Herbert.
That hee did not conceive any necessity in proceeding to debate or condemnation of the iudgment of shipmoney upon new argumentes but upon sight of the Records to iudge whether it were not aiudgment against the acts of the house, & against the petition of Right.[1]

---

[1] For the report of the Committee of Elections on 18 April, see below, **p.201**.

[Monday, 20 April]

Munday the 20th.

Mr. Bridgman.
That noe more returnes be made but two: by a sheriffe or one in two
the clerke of the Crowne to receive none but from an officer.

Sir walter Earle.
Report of the Select Committee. That petitions referred to a Select
Committee.[1] Ordered. ~~The knigghts of all shires that have presented greivances.~~[2]

mr. Grymston.
That 2 members may be called in.

Sir Hugh Chalmley.
That our goodes may not be taken by Sheriffes during the time wee
are heere in the house.

Mr. Pym.
The business of this Day that wee should proceed upon the way wee
are put in.

p.24 Sir Iohn wray.
Present greivances. 3 Heads,[3] many sandy loads of heavy oppressions,
spirituall head, spirituall Swoord, sheild. The drayners: to be represented to the greivances.[4]

Mr. Treasurer.
Report.[5] The select Committee mett sat.[6]
1. The fact: related by Mr. Lewkner. Woords read query before. That
it should be adiourned till the morrowe Seavennight.

---

[1] A select committee for Grievances was appointed on 20 April to consider '... Petitions
delivered into this House, or to be delivered from several Countries, and for all other
Grievances as any member of this House shall present' (*C.J.*, II, p.7).
[2] Erased.
[3] A source in Professor Cope's *Proceedings* (pp.227–28) lists the three heads as shipmoney,
fen drainage, and trained bands, and places the speech on 2 May, when Wray presented
'the grievances of the Countie of Lincoln'. Aston's account of the proceedings of 2 May
has no speech by Wray, which strengthens the argument that the speech took place on
20 April (Cope, p.306).
[4] I.e., to the committee for Grievances.
[5] The House here resumes the debate begun on 18 April, concerning the dissolution
of the parliament of 1629. See above, **pp.16–23**
[6] The committee appointed on 18 April.

2. That the speaker would not put the question test Sir Ionn wray & Sir walter Earle[1] done by the Kings Command. Kings declaration 1628 read.[2]

Folio 37th. Resolved to adiourne received in higher house. Absolute power declared: The Kings premptory Command to adiourne & repayre to the king.

Mr. wallor.
Moves to desert it.

Mr. pymm.
To treat of our Libertyes as englishmen, not to abridge our selves, but to put it to the question whether a breach of priveledge.

Mr. Lentall.
That wee should declare of the matter of fact & not admitt of the excuse.

Mr. Glyn.
That wee should put it to the question whether a greivance.

p.25 Mr. Herbert.
Inclination to goe to a question. To goe on cleere groundes for fact, or cleere groundes for right.
1. For fact: the speakers not obeying the house if hee did disobey the house, query if the house did command what unanimously by the whole house, query if not agreed by the house.
2. For the Kinges right. Never a greater question put in the house whether when & in what way the king can adiourne. If indefinitely wee conclude the king in a great prerogative as ever was.

Mr. Saint Iohn.
Does not Conceive any weight. Being but of fact in the speaker. If adiourned then it must be under the Seale. If meerly the kings verball woord, noe adiournment. Disputed whether a Command under the great Seale were a lawfull adiournment.

My Lord Digby.
By way of dispatch. Not question what his majestie may doe. But agree it was done & resort to the Lords.

[1]Wray and Erle both suffered imprisonment for some months in 1627 for refusing to co-operate with the forced loan. Keeler, p.166; *DNB*.
[2]This is probably the king's declaration showing the causes of the late dissolution, which can be found in Rushworth, I, App. I.

Sir Frances Seymor.
That noe one man did Contradict. Right not Contradicted: not to
goe looke for presidents wheever the Constant practize of the house
has bin otherwise.

Sir Richard Dyer.
Whether it be a question fit to be put. That this power noe more then
hee & his father exercised without exception.

p.26 Mr. Iones.
Those that dispute the Kings power this way declyne the Kings
prerogative of the power not to be disputed, but *de modis*. The [*sic*].

~~Mr. Glynn.~~[1]

Sir Henry Mildmay.
The priveledges not to be broke by our selves; when a man hath spoke
once to a question, hee ought to speake noe more.

Mr. Glynn.
To dispute of the kinges power, but the fact that he did it. If the king
himself.

Sergeant Godbolt.
If in Lawe our inferior Courts adiourned by a Comission, this Higher
ought much more.

Sir Thomas German.
That [*sic*].

Mr. Ball.
That it ought to be disputed.

Mr. Holbourne.
The king did not adiourne actually. If he can adiourne it must be in
person in both the houses. That wee ought to preserve our right by
our clayme.

Sir miles Fleetwood.
The priveledge of the parlament the life of a parlament.

[1]Erased.

Sergeant wyld.
Difference twixt upper & lower house: they sit in right of themselves
& can make a proxy, wee cannot.

Sir Iohn Davers.
Question upon the Consequence. To declare as wee conceive of greivance.

p.27 Mr. Hambden.
Noe Committee will determine what the house will not declare to be
a greivance.

Mr. Kerton.
Query whether a greivance or noe greivance.

Mr. Waller.
Likes this way because out of the way. The other, a way of modesty.

Mr. pym.
Called him to the Barr.

Sir peeter Ham[*mon*].
That wayes or query remonstrance or protestation.

Grymston.
That tis execution before iudgment.

Mr. Lewkner.
To chooze a Committee, the opinion of the Committee whether the
whole body of the house be of the opinion of the Committee.

Vaughan.
That there may be a resolution what the particulars are.

Mr. Hambden.
Whether after a verball Command to adiourne the house & the house
not adiourned it be a breach of priveledge to deny to put to the
question.

Sir Iohn Stangewayes.
That the question be made whether the Kings majesties name be put
in or noe: resolved upon the question.

Mr. Harbert [*sic*].

Sir Roger Twisden.
That hee heard his father say that the house was adiourned by the King.

Mr. Saint Iohn.
That Sir Thomas Hobby[1] vouched that the house after Command, of adiournement.

[Tuesday, 21 April]

p.28 Tuesday.[2]

Mr. pymm.
That Records being sent for out of the Kings Bench it was alleadged that the Records must be brought by the chief Iustice. Order that not waving the priveledge of the house (president being vouched that a chief Iustice had brought them) Coppyes should be taken & sent.[3]

Ordered in the house that a witnes[4] may be sent for to the committee of religion being upon the same matter.

Mr. Rigby.
That when matter is in one petition concerning severall Committees to be ended by one.

Mr. pymm.
2ds it, that if a thing in the Committee of Religion be presented, which is coincident to religion, as a petition preferd about organs & Altars: & then involved a Complaynt concerning the oath *ex officio* which, related to Courts of Iustice it should being coincident to the rest, be examyned theere.

Sir Robert Harlowe.
Preferd a petition from one peter Smart. Mr. Speaker observed it was

---

[1]Possibly Sir Thomas Posthumus Hoby.
[2]The afternoon of 21 April was spent in conference with the Lords at the Banqueting House. See below, **p.31.**
[3]Aston may have conflated Pym's remarks about the King's Bench and the Lord Chief Justice made on 20 April with his remakrs here. Copies of the records of King's Bench were ordered to be produced on 21 April. *C.J.*, II, p.7; see also Cope, pp.199–200.
[4]A Dr. Hurske. See *C.J.*, II, p.7.

not signed & theerfore not to be accepted.[1] A message to the house to meete the King at whytehall, in the Banqueting house at one a clock.

Mr. Secretary.[2]
A message to the house to meete the king at Whytehall, in the Banqueting house at one a clock.

p.29 Sir Roger North.
To the Bill for apparell that it may be Committed. Name Committee. The chequer chamber wednesday at 2 a clock.

Mr. Crewe.
Power to the Committee of religion to send for wittnesses.[3]

Mr. Speaker.
Another Bill to prevent Common recoveryes by infants.[4]

Mr. Baker.
To be enlarged for fynes.

Mr. maynard.
Mitigation to pay his fathers debts that will open a gap: to let out the Lawe.

Sir walter Earle.
To the orders of the house, if a Bill be 2nd read & cryed to be Committed, it should be referd to a committee.

Mr. Harbert.
That many may speake to a Bill heere that may not be at the Committee. If passe generall danger to overthrowe the past presidents.

Mr. Lenthall.
That the Bill is for the future.

The Records of chancery brought in. The officers examyned by the Speaker onely. A petition signed. About the receiving of Subsidies by Treasurers apoynted:[5] & ordered to take account of the Auditors, & power to send for them.

---

[1]Peter Smart, prebendary of Durham. His petition was signed later that day, but deferred until the next day. C.J., II, p.8. See below, **pp.30, 31–32.** Cf. Cope, p.199.
[2]Probably the elder Sir Henry Vane. C.J., II, p.8.
[3]'Ordered, all Committees of the whole House to have Power to send for parties' (C.J., II, p.8).
[4]Committed. C.J., II, p.8.
[5]The petition was referred to a committee (C.J., II, p.8).

p.30 Mr. Secretary windebank.
Report from the Lords about the fast, that they will agree of a time.[1]

Sir Robert Harlowe.
Got the hand to the petition & would have had it read; but denied.[2]
Records out of the star chamber about ship money.

Sir walter Earle.
The speaker to take direction from the house, to make questions.

The proceedinges in Chequer brought in by the clearkes. A Catalogue of them. Records of Common pleas brought in. The Case of the Iudges opinion about ship money. Recorded in chancery, not brought in.

Mr. Treasurer.
That the proceedings at Counsell table may be brought in.

Mr. Harbert.
It should first be resolved what to doe before wee name a Committee for that of the booke, of Table. Ill Consequences to ask things the king will not grant, they should not have. Query president for it.

Mr. pymm.
Declines the booke & moves that the sheriffes may bring in the letters sent to them from the Board. **p.31** A Committee to examyne the Records, or take coppyes & to report them: to meete This afternoone about 4 a clock.

Mr. Massall.
A motion concerning Currency by a merchant. That hee had bin 8 yeares in prizon & £2000 woorths of goods throwne away without resitution.

Order that the records concerning Bates his Case & Massalls be brought in.

Sir Iohn Stranewayes.
Move that wee meete heere to attend the Speaker to the King.

---

[1] It is not clear in the *Commons Journal* that the report from the Lords concerns a fast (*C.J.*, II, p.8).
[2] Peter Smart's petition. See above, **p.28**; below, **pp.31–32.**

Mr. Hambden.
That the Committees attend theyr course after the message heard.[1]

After noone attended the King & the Keeper made a speech. The King in person.[2]

[Wednesday, 22 April]

Mr. pym.
Leave for Sir Thomas Cheeke to depart the house for a fewe dayes upon a sad occasion.

Sir Iohn Davers.
Movd that a petition preferd yesterday may be read.[3]

Peeter Smart's petition:[4]
Bishope Iames dead.[5] Neale[6] erected an altar. One Coape 40s. One usd for fooles coate. Tooke away morning prayer at Durham. Singing with instruments. 53 pictures: 200 wax candles on Candlemas night in honor of our Lady. Preaching in a Coape. Dr. Cozens[7] preached that when they tooke away the masse tooke away religion.[8] **p.32** Publikly mayntained that the King was not supreame head of the head of [sic] Church; nor had noe more to doe in Ecclesiastical matters then he that rubbed his horses heeles.[9] Petitioner preached against the Same,[10] convented High commission, put to the oath ex officio,

---

[1]See C.J., II, p.8.
[2]Marginal note: '(Lib. A. 2)'. The Commons and Lords met in the afternoon in the Banqueting House at Whitehall. Aston does not give an account of the conference. For the speaker's report of the Lord Keeper's speech, see below, **pp.34–37.**
[3]The petition was deferred because it was unsigned. See above, **pp.28, 30.**
[4]For the text of Smart's petition, see Cope, pp.280–82. For an earlier petition against Cosin's liturgical irregularities, see the petition of Thomas Ogle. C.D. 1629, pp.124, 128.
[5]William James, Bishop of Durham (1606–1617) was Smart's patron. DNB; Mervyn James, Family, Lineage and Civil Society (Oxford, 1974), pp.118–19, 168–69, 171.
[6]Richard Neile, archbishop of York, was bishop of Durham from 1617 to 1628.
[7]John Cosin. At the time to which the petition refers he was a prebend of Durham and a royal chaplain. DNB; John G. Hoffman, 'The Arminian and the Iconoclast: The Dispute Between John Cosin and Peter Smart', Historical Magazine of the Protestant Episcopal Church (September, 1979).
[8]Cosin's text was the parable of the tares (Matthew 13:24–30). Cope, p.281.
[9]'... [Cosin] instanced oft these words that in a public meeting he shold affirme the King was not supreme head of the church: that in Excommunicacions the King had noe more authority then his man that rubbed his horses heeles ...' (C.D. 1629, p.174). See also C.D. 1629, pp.43–44, 130–31, 133, 174–77.
[10]The sermon was published: The Vanitie and Downe-fall of Superstitious Popish Ceremonies (Edinburgh, 1628).

remanded to yorke, excommunicated, degraded, find £700, imprisoned. Dr. [Cosin] Indited, convented, yet made chaplain.[1] That your petitioner hath bin kept in prizon X yeares. Lost all his estate. Now 12 months cloze prizoner.

Mr. pym.
Mooves for a Committee to pase the orders &c. to prove this petition.

Mr. Hambden.
That wee may send to enquyre by what authority he lyes in restraynt.

Mr. Secretary.
That it is by the Kings Command.

Sir Iohn Hotham.
That somebody be sent to see by what order, for that in the petition of Right *permandatum Domini Regis* is much disputed.

A Committee named to examyne & Report meete at 5 a clock.[2]

Mr. pymm.
That wee should be wary how to admitt any thing to be reported from the king but what he approves to be his.

Mr. Treasurer & windebanck.
That Report ever hath bin made by the speaker. If mistake then will be time to enquyre.

Sir walter Earle.
By the orders, noe report to be made, this irregularity, & ever brought in writing.

p.33 Speaker.
Thankes for the Care of his person. It was a Burthen too great to report a Kings woordes.

---

[1]Cosin was indicted and convicted by the Durham assizes in 1629. He received a pardon under the Great Seal. *DNB.* His activities, publications, and pardon received a good deal of attention in the parliament of 1628–1629. See *C.D. 1628*, II, pp.86nn. 46 & 51, pp.87, 89, 93, III, pp.30n. 41, 151n. 53, IV, pp.197, 207, 215, 224, 237n.7, 280n.3; *C.D. 1629*, pp.36, 37, 41, 43–47, 52, 59, 60, 124, 125, 126, 128, 130–32, 133, 139–40, 174–77, 179–80, 181, 192, 193, 246. See also Russell, *1621–1629*, p.404.

[2]See *C.J.*, II, pp.8–9. Smart's petition was represented|on the first day of the Long Parliament (November 3, 1640). *C.J.*, II, p.25. See also D'Ewes (Notestein), p.21 and in the index under *Smart, Peter*.

Mr. pymm.
Not except against the Report but that wee may have it safe, the notes
shewed the king.

Mr. Solicitor.
If the King commands attendance to receive & heare, hee himselfe
commands once & twice. More import then thought of from Nature;
Refers The same thing insubstance it requyres speedy supply. Looze
time to debate the thing informality [*sic*] to put it upon him to send
it in writing.

Mr. Speaker.
I will not surprize you in this, I will serve the house as this house
deserves to be served.

Mr. waynsford.
Our hearts are full let noe delay be.

Mr. vaughan.
Query whether a Command, to give account or to Report it to the
house. Every man heares the king aswell as wee, noe command from
the house, for the other doubtfull.

Mr. Hyde.
That hee heard the King say when you have reported, I expect an
account.

Mr. Ball.
Did not heare command for report but to expect a report. When
speaker & house together noe use of a Report. When 4 times delivered
his majesties Command noe man to spend time & dispute forme. That
wee have not yet spent our time well.

Mr. Crewe.
Noe reazon but feare of mistakes, but query either such as may
preiudice the house or the King. Wee heare regard the house: those
neere the chayre, those will take Care for the King.

p.34 Mr. Hambden.
If wee displease the house, wee displease the king. What wee take
reported cannot be amended, wee Concluded. Put it upon the speaker,
if hee will take it upon himselfe.

Mr. Controwler.
Rayze all doubts that may be. Wee that were present may helpe.

Mr. Speaker.
Consider what it concernes, the king, the house, himselfe. The greatest
honor I ever looke to have is the opinion of my fidelity to serve the
house.

Report.
The Lord Keeper: by his majesties Command put us in mynd that
the begining, the causes of this parlament were assistance & supply
in as great causes as weighty as ever to have that.
2. that if not speedy, noe use.
Reazons: that the Army was a foote & marching, that it cost £100000
a month. That if supply not proportionable, designe lost. Chardges
already bin cast away.
Quality & quantity, not for the whole woorke but to keepe that on
foote, & that spent from being lost.
Designe founded in reazons of state, to the preservation of us all.
Assur'd us in his majesties name & Royall woord, would give free
scope to present all our grevances heare them & give such an answeare
as all the kingdome should ioy in. **p.35** Then Shipmoney in particular.
That his majestie never had a thought to make a revenewe. Never to
imploy to himselfe but to the good of the people for the honor safety
& splendour of the English nation. That if not wee might by this time
have felt the woe: this to his intention, practiz'd answear able that *de
facto* he had not made any private benefit by shipmoney. That he
had added out of his owne Coffers. That wee might come to certaine
·knowledge. That the money was all delivered to Sir William Russell
Treasurer accounts to the Counsell table wheere it might appeare.
Then to particular shipwritts non [*sic*]. That his majestie did intend
none should issue but waighty afaires mov'd him from his intentions.
Reasons:
[*1.*] Necessary to prepare an army to reduce his subiects.
2. In this yeare all neighbour princes preparing strength in shipping.
3. Trade the causes of flourishing which would be lost without
defence.
4. Argeers [Algiers] 60 ships, taken Rebecca belonging to london
woorth £260000.[1] **p.36** Future, not to enrich himselfe by it [ship
money]. Desir'd to be enabled to live like a king of england, to defend
us both at home & abroad in such proportion as noe true english
heart but would wish theyr king to live. Property of goods & liberty,

---

[1]Algierian pirates were a well known danger to English shipping. See *CSPD*, 1637–
1638, pp.15, 192, 219, 243, 605, 607.

hee would be as willing [as] wee to have, as wee to ask. Wayes to make this the happyest parlament that ever was. Advize that it might be soe. Appoynt us the way by putting an obligation of trust & consideration upon the king which should secure us more then any thing wee could possibly propose. Reazon, good manners the way, that the honor of being trusted by his people be priz'd above all thinges, & scorned to be over come by kindnes by his people. That Ireland before the 2d day last parlament gave 6 Subsidies. Trusted on his woord & promise, that they had all granted with advantage. That this instant parlament had given supply accompanyed with an expression as great as the grant that was woorth 50 or £60000. **p.37** Reioyced in that, more in this as his dearest Kingdome. This principally to the Commons as the proper way of supply. But had calld the Lords to be wittnesses, as ready to Concur with then. That his majestie would expect a speedy account. Answer objections of Tonnadge & pondage as for defence for noe ship money. That was ordeined for usuall preservation not for extraordinary. Prevent others strength & strike terror into them. That he had forgott shipmoney. That if shipmoney were not fit, fynd another way, safe iust & honorable his majestie would accept it. That his majestie did expect his Report & a quick account.

Mr. Kerton.
Noe man but desirous to make this happy parlament. This weighty, wee many great & weighty. Motions to put the house into a Committee & not to stop till something resolved.

Mr. Goodwin.[1]
That as he could not forbeare the shipmoney, soe hee expected the Concurrence of the house to assist the Gathering.

Mr. pymm.
To refer till to morrowe morning.

Mr. Crewe.
I was for a present Report but not for a suddain resolution which wee thinke the king does not expect.

Mr. Controwler.
Enter into the debate to day, shewe alacrity to.

[1]Probably Ralph Goodwin.

p.38 Mr. purfray.
Not to be lock'd up by our owne orders but to proceed as wee see occasion.

Mr. Hambden.
Diff[*erence*] about the order call in the messengers, then consider of the order.

Sir George W[*entworth*].
Would have the woord good resolution.

Judges Bramston & Foster sent from Lords. King pleazed with the Fast, Lords desire a Conference about time & Circumstances. After noone about 3 a clock in painted chamber. Number appointed of them 12. Speaker repeates it to the house.

Mr. pym.
Answer noe long debate. They 12, wee double the Number. Judges calld in to receive this answer. Sergeant still fetches his Mace. Not speake till the mace layd downe.

Sir walter Earle.
Gravity of the house reserved at the first & 2d congee [*sic*] not to moovd. 3d. Speaker mooves.

Mr. pym.
At entrance those at the Barr put of theyr hatts, as they ascend others. At the Table the speaker, & not at going out till they be at the last at going out. The speaker puts not of his hat whyles he speakes to them. Name the 24.

p.39 Sir Robert Harlowe.
That a message mooving from us to the Lords, wee are to make a draught.

Mr. pym & Sir waler [*sic*] Earle.
That being to consider of Circumstances. Wee are to have eares only. Order that Kings declaration, Reported delayed till to morrowe & to be debated of as long as cause shall requyre.

Mr. Holburne.
Report of a Commission to the Convocation issued, not enrowled, not by ordinary way of privy Seale but immediat warrant from the king.[1]

---

[1]For further reading on the subject of the king's prerogative to issue a warrant to Convocation, see Esther Cope, 'The Short Parliament of 1640 and Convocation', *Journal of Ecclesiastical History* (April, 1974), pp.168, 173–76.

That Commission was granted to treat of altring exposition of ould, or making newe Cannons.

Sir Ralph Hopton.
With a good will. Doubt. Great debate. Wee were in a way.

Mr. pym.
Every petition presents innovation in religion, That noe ordinance be made by the clergy, without the Concurrence of this house. R.2:5 cleargy agree in Convocation the Lords consent, the commons deny it. The statute repealed & Cancelled. Consider how assembled by neither by the pope by the ArchByshop, but by writt of parlament. Moove for order That the Lords & wee may move his majestie that noe such commission may be executed till the house adiudged of it.

p.40 Mr. Harbert.
Too much hast to order it. Of the mynd preserve the honor of this house & the liberty of Conscience. But see a fresh example. Of the dignity of the house, a busines of this weight from the King, if upon mention of 2 presidents, which are not seene if not on implicite fayth, bring them, read them. Till seene, weight advise on debate, then goe to the Lords, when seene.

Mr. Saint Iohn.
To the order not to be diverted wee doe but offer inconveniences. Presidents summons of parlaments, where to treat of *ad tractandum et consultandum* the Convocation comes likewise, by direction *ad consentiendum* in query *de communi consilio regni*. They can but consent the Commons to treat. If otherwise, wheeres our liberty if they may make Cannons [?], excommunication must followe, then hath he no property in his estate. If his goods outed he cannot plead, if his person taken a writt *ex commuincato capiendo*. Anselmes time. In the popes time his cannons did not bynd the subiect. Kings booke that he would never give way to innovation in religion. But preserve it as established in Queen Elizabeths time.[1] Presently to [repair] to the Lords.

p.41 Mr. Herbert.
Motion. Not suffer him to speake having spoke allready.

Mr. Iones.
Not fitt to goe to the Lords yet, either generall or particulars. Move that my Lord keeper may shewe his commission that will be a ground.

---

[1]Possibly a reference to 'A proclamation for the establishing of the peace and quiet of the Church of England, 16 June 1626'. *Foedera*, XVIII, pp.719–20.

Mr. Den.
Offers a letter from Sir Thomas Rowe,[1] twas said the churches beyond
Sea, were about to forsake us because wee are about to forsake our
owne religion. Calld on to name them.

Sir Ralph Hopton.
To qualify them.

Mr. vaughan.
That there might be a mistake because hee sayd hee did but conceive
hee heard them.

Mr. Treasurer.
The glory of a wise man to passe by an offence, much lesse soe many
wise men. Never knew a member mistake a woord, & offer to explane
himselfe but hee was admitted. The Commission to be seene. Whoe
knowes the effect of it. The Reporters could not fynd it. Wee are noe
court of Record, wee must take information, must wee goe upon one
petition. Desires things may passe affirmatively, not negatively by
opposition.

Mr. Hambden.
That the woords not to be conceived by him alone but by some man
ells. If explayned hee may excuse him selfe, but it lyes still on the
members.[2]

p.42 Sir walter Earle.
Wrong to the Iustice of the house to let such a thing fall.

Mr. Den.
Himselfe confessed that hee conceived the woords to fall from mr.
pymm.

Mr. pymm.
That hee sayd [sic].

Mr. Hambden.
In respect hee was never heere before. If hee by the vote of the house
be satisfyed in his iudgment that hee was mistaken, hee may declare
soe & aske forgivenes.[3]

---

[1]Probably Sir Thomas Roe, ambassador, who sat in the Long Parliament for the
University of Oxford. *DNB*.
[2]Another source attributes a similar remark to Pym. Cf. Cope, p.169.
[3]Another source attributes a similar remark to Pym, not Hampden. Cf. Cope,
p. 169. However, 'Mr. Dell ... had been brought to ye barre but for Mr. Hampden
his friend' (Cope, p.246).

Mr. pymm.
That the Commission may be againe treated of.

Mr. Glynn.
To have time till to morrowe morning.

Mr. Grimston.
The skill of a phisition to apply preventing phisick. Therefore to the Lords.

Mr. Controwler.
Quintilians Counsell: that they that had the power to procure this Commission will have power to preserve it.

Mr. Wyn.
That the popes imposed Cannons breach excommunication: unlesse fact appeare first, how shall wee proceed.

Sergeant wyld.
What ground not seeing Commission. But by the effect wee see the Ground: if noe more but Fame, it were enough.

Mr. Bridgman.
Profitt not for matter unlesse wee knew what it were. Concerning the King by his Seale. Move to delay it till morning.[1]

p.43 Mr. Holbourne.
How far a Cannon may bynd, not to be disputed on a suddain. Wheere more cleere cannot be had wee may proceed: wheere wee may & in a day. It is fitt to see the Commission, or Coppy.

Mr. Flood.
That wee have the Commission distinctly & ioyned with the Lords.

Sir waler [*sic*] Earle.
Noe man comes in a mynd to mistake. Not to enter upon the Bulke of the Busines but to put a stop to the in iustice of the proceeding & to put it to the question.

Mr. Ball.
Hastning without sight will retard it.

---

[1]Bridgeman was the son of the bishop of Chester.

Mr. Dyett.
Because concerning power, his majestie & they can make no cannon that can bynd the subiect without consent in parlament.

Mr. Alstree.
Noe dispute of the Cannons power; the kings power. But matter of fact.

Sir Iohn Strangwayes.
Resolution in this howse. That Common Fame is a ground to enquyre on or to transfer it to the king or Lords. 1626 it was soe voted.[1] Theerfore the sooner the better.

Sir Edward Cooke.[2]
The Lords Already rize, wee cannot goe to the lords. If in the meane time the Committee may see the Records against to morrowe.

p.44 Order: Noe man ought to goe out when a question is propounded.

Mr. Harbert.
If wee will goe to the question wee must state a particular what wee goe upon.

Mr. Treasurer.
Information to the house ere wee goe upon it: Remember what happned upon Common fame. But first upon enquyry.

Sir walter Earle.
To the question not upon Common Fame.

Sir Iohn Strangewayes.
More then Common fame. Grounds enough given.

Mr. Rowse.
It cannot be calld 'common fame', which every man knowes of innovations in religion.

Sir Henry mildmay.
That wee put the question wrong, the Lords being up, upon an impossibility. The matter not knowne on an uncertainty.

---

[1]In the spring of 1626, the Commons proceeded against the duke of Buckingham on the grounds of 'common fame'. Roger Lockyer, *Buckingham: The Life and Political Career of George Villiers, First Duke of Buckingham* (London, 1981), p.320; *C.J.*, I, pp.847, 849–852.
[2]Probably a mistake on Aston's part for Sir Robert Cooke.

Sir miles Fletwood. [*sic*]

Sir phillip manwaring.
2 hares on Foote, the generall that wee goe to the Lords, particularly whether to the Lords presently it is impossible, if to morrowe, wee goe lame.

Mr. vaughan.
Going to the Lords. Noe such question as will not stand with the creditt of the house. If wee goe to the Lords the subiect not resolved, wee iudge the question our selves.

p.45 Sir Ralph Hutton.
Wee cannot doe it to day, what consequence. Wee must goe upon petitions which is referd to the Committee, can we goe before the Committee report.

Mr. Brerwood.
The Commission may be drawne with limitation to referr to the approbation of the house of commons, then wee complaine without cause.

Query Mr. Lewkner.
This house great Counsell of ye kingdom. Proceed with gravity & moderation. Whether ground sufficient, if noe other way that way. But being of noe use why such hast. [Common] fame cause sufficient, hope more feare then cause. That the Convocation mooved that they might doe something *non Synodice Sileamur*. Confesse that they have the Commission & in it are severall restrictions. Query. To goe to the Lords to petition against innovation in Religion. The same Committee which was before enlardgd by some fewe. Today at 3 a clock to prepare the Conference with the Lords.

[Thursday, 23 April]

p.46. Thursday: 23[d].

The fast resolved.[1] Saturday come sevennight. The preachers chozen by vote.[2] A Committee to keepe a note of those that receive & to keepe the money usually collected.

[1]See above, **p.38.**
[2]The preachers appointed for Saturday were Richard Holdsworth, master of Emmanuel College, Cambridge, anti-Laudian and future royalist; and Stephen Marshall, vicar of Finchingfield, Essex, popular preacher for the Long Parliament and future presbyterian. Ralph Brownrig, master of St. Catherine's Hall, Cambridge, and bishop of Exeter in 1641, was intreated to preach on the next day at Holy Communion in St. Margaret's, Westminster. C.J., II, p.9; Cope, pp.237, 237n.2; *DNB*; Nalson, I, p.330.

Sir Thomas Baring[*ton*].[1]
Noe man admitted to sitt till a Certificate hee hath received the Communion.

Sir walter Earle.
That the Sergeant goe to the Bar to Summon all the Lawyers to the house that are absent.

Mr. Cage.
Motion that the Iudges give precedency of motion to the lawyers of the house that they might attend heere.

Mr. pym.
That the iudges in Care of the house will doe it.

Mr. King.
A motion made to excuse one that would question. An election; opposed by mr. pymm, that wee have discharged members that have bin sick; if he would question it hee might have sent his petition. & not leave Roome for clamors to come in.

Mr. Lenthall called to the chayre.
The order read to resolve into a Committee.

Sir Beniamin Ruddyar.
In my opinion done wisely, dutifully to the king. Let us trust him first that wee may trust him heerafter. The commonwealth is a most miserable spectacle but wee have the Kings woord for a redress, as sacred, soe it ought to be inviolable. Soe enter on this woorke, labour to bring it to a speedy happy Conclusion.

A long pauze. Noe man speaking.

p.47 Sir Ralph Hopton.
In this busines our best endeavors pleads for favour to his iust intentions though unready expression. To church & Common wealth obligation equall, to his majesties service equall to any mans. A poynt in all busines wheer unto all 3 concurr. Though sometimes a precedence the Rule alters not. In Contemp of all from king & Keeper out. I conceive that it is a duty ingraven in the hearts[2] of all to contribute a ready & dutifull obedience & not to retard for any

---

[1]Barrington and his brother-in-law Sir William Masham (Colchester) were appointed churchwardens for the Communion service to take place on Sunday, 3 May. Cope, p.237.
[2]Aston did not write the word 'hearts' but drew a small heart.

greivance, complaynt, claime, what soever which shall not carry in
its owne nature the impediment of this proper service. Explaine by
an example. If a Master comand his servant to make hast & returne
without grant of things usefull, & he make excuses, hee is too blame.
But if he have a thorne in his foote, hee must pull it out, this is noe
delay. Thornes in the feete, in the Hart, in the eye of many. Noe desire
to multiply or aggrevate them. Lord Keepers speech[1] weighty, not
sound it methodically, but hast to the last part. In it an influence of
his majesties grace as the sonne out of a cloud. Tonnadge & pondage.
Not sufficient, therfor necessary to have encrease of supply. But
declared that his majesties pleazure was, if greivous to the Common
wealth, some other Course. Propound 3 propositions. The way of
ship[*money*] & all unparliamentary supply not Servicable to the King,
profitable to the Common wealth, **p.48** onely Thornes.
1. Nothing but parliament avaylable.
I reazon: that that way of being which deiects the hearts of the
subiects, that distracts the trade, not profitable. The Revenues of the
subiect is the myne of the king[*dom*]. A Count has a field: if the ground
be rich if hee drawe not out, weeds shall suck out the heart the
Kingdom the great field. In this sense unprofitable for King, not
tollorable for the public.
2. Reason. Wheerby the drawe from Common wealth 5ˢ & bring the
King but one. Unprofitable. Shipmoney above £200000 a yeare.
Countrey cast up all by chardges in suits in references it costs the
kingdome £100000 more. If the countrey had husbanded theyr own
contribution, saved halfe the money.
2. Sort monopolies. That on the wines by a contract of £300000 *per
annum* they receive £800000.
3. Court of honor[2] which hee wantt a Commodious supply of subjects.
4. Courts Eclesiasticall. New businesses in the church as much in
valewe as the other greivances. Speedy in husbanding the Common
wealth. A vast Gulfe of infirmity & charge opening upon us. The
Gulfe of war: chardge £100000 a month. Woorth our consideration
wheere £130000 is to be had but entred into. This the ould rent of
death & desolation. Pluto faigned to come in limping & goe away
runing, this contrary. That the mother of the dead chyld should be
contented the chyld should be divided. But that the mother of the live
would keepe it whole.[3] **p.49** 2d be That the way of parlament onely
way without question satisfactory. 3d be If wee set to it, able to pull
out some of these thornes, if wee set in ioynt way, & this his motion.

[1]See above, **pp.34–37**.
[2]I.e. the Earl Marshal's court. For further reading on the 'Court of honor', see G. C.
Squibb, *The High Court of Chivalry* (Oxford, 1959).
[3]I Kings 3:16–28.

Mr. Controwler.
Wee doe not goe the way expected. Come with intention to baire the
wounds of our greivances. Not to keepe them too greene, nor cloze
them too soone. Releeve him in those occasions, must mayntayne his
honor. In point of curtesie disdayn'd to be belyed & let us trust him.
Our greivances promised. Wee have the meanes for preservation of
his honor & our safety. Expect this parlament a poynt of time, from
whence all ages have reckoned theyr felicity. Move to goe the business.

Sir Francis Seymer.
Time pretious, short: majesties supply & greivance of Common wealth
both into consideration, which precedency. Duty & affection presse
supply. The great trust of the Common wealth, too great to be
betrayed. Not to hazard meerly & wholly on future hopes. Tould us
to trust his majesties if noe more but to trust his majestie it were fitt,
but when our proceedings shalbe made by false glosse of noe use, as
in our petition of right wee have cause to feare the woorst. Move that
though our gr[ievances] numerous yet content us with fowr. **p.50** To
doe more were to neglect our trust to doe lesse, were to neglect the
king.

Sir Iohn Strangwayes.
To represent the greivances is the first parlamentary. This the place,
this the greatest Counsell. Well exprest 'a thorne in our foote'.[1] The
shipmoney thought fitt to be represented a greivance by the vote of
the house, if the King will enable us to goe wee will run. Enable us
to serve God: to searve him in our property, if the sense of the whole
house.

Sir Iohn wray.
This deserves great debate. Tis the language of us all, wee shall [*sic*].
Not the greatest monarch that can doe what he will but like God that
can doe noe wrong: wee doubt not the king as God loves cheerfull
givers.[2] Let but our french motto be cleared *Soit* &c. Wee shall doe
myracles.

Mr. Kerton.
The vote right both to serve King & Countrey. The way a Conference
with the Lords. 3 heads. Religion, property, liberty [in] parlament.

Mr. Roberts.
Move it may be put to the question.

[1]See above, **p.47**.
[2]II Corinthians 9:7.

Mr. Controwler.
Nor with the custom nor priveledges to move to the Lords, before resolution of the house be knowne.

Sir walter Earle.
If nothing but Supply, it were fitt goe to the Lords, if onely those 3 heads & wee ripe for it, put it to the question.

p.51 Mr. Solicitor.
Wee are in a Committee, & directed by order of the house. That limitts us to the direction by the King. Which was shortly thus. The great occasions opened were such as would not admitt time. How for they supply in poynt of time this day taken. Lay it aside undebated, & goe upon the same things wee were upon before. This is not such a consideration as was resolved on.

Sir Harbottle Grymstone.
Ship money now in gathering, they would all meete to gather. Wee shall have ill welcome Home.

Mr. Ball.
A question ere Ripe never succesfull. Not parlamentary way to confer with the Lords concerning the supply. A way prescribed but left to our owne liberty How.

Mr. mallary.
Wee in a ready way to come to his supply. Part of our prayer every day to shewe love to the Countrey. Till ship money taken away, I cannot give, I shall then give freely.

Mr. Treasurer.
Unhappy to have division amongst us when all those of the Roman religion are uniting. Sir Humphrey May to the King press'd the liberty of the subiect. To the people the power of the King. Hee was not nor could not be beleeved.[1] Tis knowne how unhappy the issue was.[2] Tis the countrey that must doe it.

---

[1]Sir Humphrey May (1573–1630) was MP for Leicester in 1628–1629. Two statements of Sir Humphrey's may be suggested as possible sources for the treasurer's remark. May was reported as saying on 23 February 1629: 'That we take this as highe point of previldge, and his Majestie takes it as a high point of a Soverangnety, and therefore would not have us thinke soe much of the previledge of this house as to neglect that of the Soveragnety' (Notestein, *1629*, p.169). Another possibility is May's letter to Thomas Wentworth on 27 December 1627. See Russell, *1621–1629*, p.340. I am grateful to Professor Russell for bringing the latter to my attention.
[2]I.e. the dissolution of the 1628–1629 parliament.

p.52 Mr. Glynn.
Negative that it is not whether wee may give Supply or noe. But whether before or after; must goe hand in hand. Reazon of Supply first. Some good Angel hath stirrd this poole of Bethesda, & I hope wee shall take the time to cure our deseases.[1] To drawe president when the Kingdome is wounded. A [?] duty lyes upon us, which discharge wee shall give freely.

Mr. Ball.
Onely to poynt of time that the graunt might proceed, time to passe a Bill of subsidies.

Mr. pert.
If wee must give, wee must have to give, slaves may restore, onely freemen can give. The property of our goods invaded by ship money. The King may take, wee cannot give if gathered sitting parlament. Not questioned it is a Confirmation.
2. Liberty if not that wee are tounge tyed.
3. Liberty pretious, property deare, but if I have noe religion I have them onely for the divell.

Mr. Harbert interupts.
Not fitt nor sufferable to be cald an abomination, when tis upon a iudgment. Not fitt to say if wee bee Heathens in religion.

Mr. Controwler.
If speaking of the religion of the Iudges he might have used the woord divell.

p.53 Mr. pert.
Hee did not say that wee had Heathenish religion, but hee that had noe religion was a Heathen, not a devill. Hee had an English heart, & wish'd noe man that heard him but had an English eare.

Mr. Treasurer excepted.

Mr. Harbert.
Refer it to the iudgment of the house whether if it must rest upon one, it must be voted whether it must rest upon him that had an ill tongue, or upon him that had an ill eare.

---

[1] I.e. grievances. 'For an angel went down at a certain season into the pool, and troubled the water: whoever then first after the troubling of the water stepped in was made whole of whatsoever disease he had' (John 5:4).

Sir walter Earle.
Not to rest upon such exceptions but to passe by.

Sergeant Godboult.
That the king does not demand a plenary but fitt to thinke upon a
Competency. Ship money was a dying, let us not revive it.

Mr. Hambden.
Custome of the house that any woords spoke at a committee & taken
offence at must be reported to the chayre to the whole house & theere
sentenced.

Mr. Speaker takes the chayre. & hee does retract the woords. Voted
& cleared.

Mr. pymm.
2 Things spoken of must be taken away. Impossibility & necessity, if
wee have not to give tis not possible, if wee remove not that necessity
but lay more burthens they will not be borne. Theerfore moves as a
ready way. To goe to the question.

Mr. Hyde.
When soe a neere Consent in substance wee should not differ in
circumstances. **p.54** Noe man but wishes the taking away that destructive woord 'necessity' by a free supply. 2 motions that theere may be
a Select Committee to prepare a petition soe sensible soe full a draught
as may impossesse the King of the right of it. 2^d of that of religions
the same way.
3. Enter into debate of some way of supply, which must requyre some
time, remove both Iealouzies.

Mr. secretary.
The circumstance of time, caution that if wee doe not supply the King
wee shall hardly releeve our greivances.

Mr. King.
There must be first an ability.

Mr. Grymston.
Would have us not shewe consent in vyce onely but in effect operative.
Would have both goe together. Put to the question.

Mr. pellam.
Nemo potest dare quod non habet. Theerfore desire that wee may goe to
the Lords to remonstrate.

Sir Arthur Hazelrig.
Query if not goe to the Lords immediately.

p.55 Mr. Iones.
Greife that wee are put upon such narrowe time. When wee are tould
that ship money must be taken away if this & subsidie should march
to gether, wee had a president of a great & honorable person dyed in
countenancing a subsedie in H:7th's time.[1] 21° King Iames imminent
necessity. If you doe not give declare that ye will give creditt heere &
abroad.

Sir philip manwaring.
Noe man against supply of the king. Instances the ready progresse in
Ireland.[2]

Mr. Iones.
Difference twixt the parlaments in England & Ireland. That by
conquest: holds noe proportion, theere was is & ever should be difference betwixt them.

Mr. wayntworth.
To take into consideration the present danger. Theyr wives children
& families lay exposd to it.

Mr. Kerton.
Wee must aswell consider the groanes & cryes & miseries of our
Country, & that if there be not releefe in them, the danger may be as
great in England as in Scotland.

Mr. pymm.
Promise in the petition of right. Never love bying of Iustice. The ship
money wee shall not dischardge the trust in us, if wee give any thing
before that be taken away.

Mr. persey.
Know if wee trust the kings promises or noe. Calld on to declare.

Mr. vaughan.
Without question. That without redresse wee would not give wee
could not give. If he can take at his owne pleazure, noe use of our
giving. When the King is in necessity wee are as much obliged to give
as he to redresse. **p.56** Time in debate of shipmoney. If a iudgment

[1]Henry Percy, fourth earl of Northumberland, was killed by Yorkshire rioters while
attempting to collect taxes in 1489.
[2]See above, **p.36**. Mainwaring was Stratford's secretary in Ireland.

not reversed a new writt may be revived & wee are never the nearer then but as if there had never bin a parlament. That a president the kings to goe first. Answeared that they may goe together. In the Grant of the great charter it is mentioned that such guyfts were given for & in consideration of those great things granted to them.

Sergeant Wyld.
3 sorts of necessity to the Question.

Sir Henry Martin.
Drawe us to gather. I. King supply, out of trust to the countrey they cannot doe it. Returne nothing but act of subsidie. Religion long debate. Propound that you should have somwhat presently, wee somwhat presently, neither the woorse. such an act of subsidie, as may supply London. Condition ship money be prooved lawfull then a valuable sum.

Mr. Hambden.
That that way was not parlamentary by condition. Religion as much. Property concern'd in military impositions monopolies. &c. as much as in ship money.

Mr. Harbert.
Necessary & unavoydable to make any question but how to give to the King **p.57** An account of what expected. If wee could not give the case otherwise nothing yet stated heere as a greivance.

Mr. Crewe.
The mayne not against it. Not for day, not for Conference. Against the priveledge of the house. Conference either answer or noe answer. Propose something that may give the king satisfaction. A Sub Committee to consider of Supply.

Mr. pymm.
The King hath not tyed us to dayes nor houres. Convenient that the king take noe notice of our debates till wee are come to resolution. 6°.E.3 propositions for great supply desired time to consider with the Countrey which wee desire not. Moove that upon these greivaces which disable us wee may consult with the Lords.

Sir walter Earle.
2 resolved.

Mr. Harbert.
If 2 questions on foote it must be voted to resolve which shalbe the question.

Sir Robert Harlowe.
What account till the woorke done the question to be put.

Mr. Secretary.
To declare the Kings intention. That he does expect an account presently from us.

Lord Digby.
Whether as from the King as a message or as a member of the house.

Mr. Controwler.
To delay it till to morrowe.

Mr. Flood [*sic*].

p.58 Mr. pymm.
Answer. To a declaration to be made take heed wee hurt it not. Our Consciences & our duties to our Countries bynd us, wee cannot doe it.

Mr. Ball.
Not satisfied which to be preferd first.

Mr. pryce.[1]
Alter it from religion to innovation in church discipline.

Sir peeter Hammon.
To alter it according to the order that is innovation concerning matters of religion. Concerning the priveledges of our persons for matters done in parlament. And the property of our goods. Put to the question & resolved 'I'.

Mr. Harbert.
That the affirmative being put, any of the house may speake before the Negative be put.

Speaker repayres to the chair & tis reported. Then put to the question & confirmed by the 'I'.

Mr. Hambden.
To appoynt a committee to consider of reducing the matter fitt to be presented to the Lords. A Committee named.

---

[1]Either Charles Price (Radnorshire) or Herbert Price (Breconborough). John Price, who was MP for Mountgomeryshire in the Long Parliament, was a candidate for the county seat in the spring, but was defeated by Richard Herbert. Keeler, pp.313–15; *MofP*.

[Friday, 24 April]

p.59 24th.
Lord maltravers releases arrundell.

Mr. Fines. Complaynes.
A petition of constables in oxfordshire.[1] Prizons in oxford. William walter[2] sheriffe sends warrant to distrayne, desire security from actions, refuzing, they are committed & pray releefe.[3] Refere to the Committee.

Sir Thomas Smith.
17 dayes before arested. Protestion of priveledge 16 dayes before & after, this without compasse. Proceedings to be stayed.

An act read for preventing inconveniences by occupancy. Recyt all mischeifes. If any man have land for lives noe power to dispose by will.[4] That if he dye undisposed haz by entry of a stranger to hould the occupancy. Remedy that he may have power to dispose by will or chardge it with Rent. If intestate, that the executor or administrator it shalbe in nature of chattell Lyable to debts.

Mr. King.
Honest to provide for wife & child. Debts as iust That the speciall occupant may be lyable.

Mr. Rigby.
The devisee not to be in better case then the heyre at lawe. Devise allowed but debts preferd & hee take it chargeable with the devisors debts.

Mr. maynard.
That it should be devizable, to the executors &c Inconvenience. If the lessee devize it for years, the remainder descend. What remedy the 2nd for wast. If not but fall. Executor pull down howse, wast

---

[1] The High Sheriff was Rodolph Warcopp.
[2] For the text of this petition, see Cope, p.284.
[3] 'Petition of Rodolph Warcopp, sheriff of co. Oxford, to the Council ... At the last quarter sessions in Oxford the under-sheriff warned all the bailiffs within the county to attend the sheriff at the Bear, in Oxford, there to receive directions and warrants for collecting the ship-money, but they would not come, so that all officers, both constables and bailiffs, refuse either to receive, obey, or exercise my warrants, or to assist me in this service' (*CSPD*, 1640, p.370).
[4] Marginal note: '2nd time read'.

woods, he cannot be chardged beyond assetts. Soe the Lord [*sic*] noe remedy. **p.60** If one enter & out mee, wheere contestation is *inter executor* and administrators noe remedy. Moove that it may not goe to the executors but to the heyre. If to an heyre all provided for by making him lyable to the debts, & the other mischiefes. Prevent if devisee lyable. More mischiefe, makes a stranger lyable to what he knowes not.

Sir Thomas witherington.
In case noe devise lawe provides to executor. It will come in the power of the ordinary & he incurs onely a penalty of & may give it his sonne.

Sir Thomas Bowyer.
May come into such hands as theere may be a surrender to revue the estate. Committed to: all the Lawyers. To meete at Lincolnes Inn Hall to day 3 a clock.

Mr. Iones.[1] Report.[2]
Mr. chadwell, Mr. Courtney[3] returned. Basset & one other Complayned.[4] That 1 had 13. The others 24. Exceptions to the precept choze the same day by maior part of free Burgers, 19 in all. One 11, other 13. All personall notice but 2 debate whether Burgers alone or inhabitants. Appeard that all the inhabitants did assent though they had noe right. That if it had bin a great towne & inhabitants many might be surprizd. But 35 inhabitants in all & 28 at election. Agreed lawfull.[5] Except to the returne because the port reave & Burgeses, the port reave being but for a yeare. But overruled because the new one was not sworne.

p.61 Sir Henry Compton,[7] mr. whyte,[7] mr. Goodwyn.[8]
For East Grimsteed in Sussex. Petition by towne that the right was in the Burgage holders. That Goodwin gayned voyces wher had noe

[1]Charles Jones. Hirst, p.78.

[2]Aston's account of the disputed election in St. Michael is confused. See below, **p.212**; *C.J.*, II, p.10; Mary Coate, *Cornwall in the Great Civil War and Interregnum* (Truro, 2nd edn., 1963), pp.18, 23–24; Keeler, p.39.

[3]Peter Courteney and William Chadwell, MPs for Michael. Keeler, p.131; *MofP*.

[4]Francis Basset and Samuel Coseworth were also returned for the borough of Michael in Cornwall. See Hirst, p.61; *MofP*.

[5]Marginal note: 'Question resolved "I" '.

[6]Sir Henry Compton (East Grinstead); *AO*.

[7]John White (Rye); Keeler, pp.390–91. Though disputing Robert Goodwin's election for East Grinstead, White was also returned for Rye, sitting for the latter in both parliaments of 1640.

[8]Robert Goodwin (East Grinstead) Keeler. pp.191–92.

right.[1] All choze Sir Henry Compton, hee returnd duely. Mr. whyte 13. Goodwin 14. 7 noe Burgers because made a conveyance to multiply voyces. Noe fraud for it was in execution of a legacy & treated before. Retort the same exception.

Goodwin proves the inhabitants to have voyces.

Reply: when noe competition. But indentures returned by Burgers & others Inhabitants. An Indenture 1°: Marie. 36.H.8. Returned by Bayliffe Burgers, & other inhabitants. Soe Mr. Goodwin elected by 31 Adiudged. A Baylyffe which is but a Baylyffe of a Lord & noe sworne officer. The Comminalty without them. That the Bayliffe[2] threatned all that did not give voyces his Lord should take notice of them. That after were threatned coming to witnes that hee would Billet 6 men upon them & theyr sonnes should be sent to beare Armes.

Voted & Resolved. Both good Elections.

Sir Ralph Hopton.
That it might be passd by. But twas resolved as a delinquent. An Indenture concerning Edward Ascough[3] not return'd in Lincolneshire.

Mr. pelham.
That if men lawfully elected shalbe put out the sheriffe may put out any man. That the [sic].

p.62 Mr. maynard.
Wheere 2 Indentures return'd by the sheriffe, if any man put an Indenture into the Sheriffes hands whoe is a sworne officer wee put out all the members of the house.

Mr. Sergeant Fynch.
That it should be return'd.

Mr. Hyde.
That the sheriffe should send it in. Not returned.

---

[1] It was White who promoted the petition accusing Goodwin of appealing for support beyond the traditional franchise. Fletcher, *Sussex*, pp.244–45; *C.J.*, II, p.10.

[2] Edward Blundell, the earl of Bristol's bailiff. *C.J.*, II, p.10; Fletcher, *Sussex*, p.245.

[3] Sir Edward Ayscough of South Kelsey, Lincolnshire, later sat for the county in the Long Parliament, but was defeated in his bid to unseat his rival Sir Edward Hussey for the seat in the spring. On this day Ayscough's indenture was called to be examined by the Committee for Privileges. *C.J.*, II, p.10; Keeler, pp.55, 93–94; *MofP*.

Mr. pymm.

In case of Leicester Indenture return'd. Iustified the returne that hee would not returne because hee was noe freehoulder nor resient [*sic*]. Soe he was ordered by the house which dischardges his penalty by the statute.[1]

Sir Thomas witherington.

That it may be brought in foorth with to the Committee of priveledges.

Questiond & 'I'.

Goodwynn of Northampton.

A petition.[2] Alexander Iennings an assessor for ship money. Sent for to the Lords, prizon 2 yeares, for denying shipmoney. Bound in £1000 to attend yet was sent to the prizon agayne. Bound to the good behaviour. Brought action of false imprizonment, atturney sent for & not released without Fees.

Mr. Fynes.

A difference betwixt things done by writ & what without Coulour of the writ. In such Case the house may looke upon them as delinquents. Noe warrant to put them in the Iayle for not distrayning.

Mr. Speaker.

Except in breach of priveledge noe man in lardged.

Mr. pymm.

In a Breach of Common Lawe it is to goe to the Lords & there releese to be resolved.

p.63 Mr. Hambden.

Whether in Conference with the Lords about the ship money. These petitions may not be taken into Consideration; that if it appeare they are onely imprizond, for this & noe things ells they may have releese.

Messegers returne from the Lords.

---

[1]Probably a reference to the case of Roger Smith of Edmonton, who was chosen in March 1640, along with Simon Every of Egginton, burgess in parliament for Leicester. Smith informed the mayor that he could not assent to take the oath of a freeman. Consequently, he was disqualified from serving and Thomas Coke of Gray's Inn was chosen in his place. James Thompson, *The History of Leicester* (Leicester, 1849), p.359; Keeler, p.54.

[2]The petition was referred to committee. *C.J.*, II, p.11.

Godfrey.

That a petition being lost, a newe may preferd to come in the same order.[1]

Mr. Secretary windebanck.[2]

Lords Busie, & they send when at better leizure.

The 2 cheife Iustices without as messengers from the Lords. Sergeant brings them in.

Bramston.[3]

The Lords thankes for the message [concerning a joint committee], excuse because entred debate of busines of weight, by Kings presence. Repeated by the Speaker.

Sir walter Earle. Report.

Of the inducement of the reazons of Conference with the Lords. Mett Court of wards. Sate late. Mett to day Committee chamber 7 a clock.

3 heads: particulars many read them.

I.[4]

1. The Commission to the convocation house by reazon innovations thence.

2. By reason petitions against innovation out of Counties.

3. Molesting ministers conformable without warrant of lawe.

4. Publishing popish tenents in bookes, disputations.

5. Restrayning ministers preaching in theyr owne chardges.

[2] Goods.[5]

2 [1]. Monopolies & restraint of trade.

[2] Shipmoney.

3. Forrests beyond bounds.

4. Coate & Conduct money. Wages, armes, horses & carts.

p.64 5. Denying releefe in Courts of Iustice.

6. Imprizonment for denying monopolies &c. Unwarrantable taxes.

---

[1]Probably a reference to the petition of Daniel White of Winchelsey, Sussex. It was delivered to a committee on 18 April and mislaid. The house ordered that a new petition may be preferred '... and that it may be admitted as exhibited upon *Saturday* last: And so it is ordered' (*C.J.*, II, p.11).

[2]'Mr. Secretay *Windebank* went up with a Message to the Lords, concerning a Fast, according to the Order Yesterday' (*C.J.*, II, p.10). See above, **p.46**.

[3]Sir John Bramston, Chief Justice, Court of King's Bench. *D.NB*.

[4]'I. Concerning Innovation in Matter of Religion' (*C.J.*, II, p.11).

[5]'II. Concerning Propriety of Goods' (*C.J.*, II, p.11). The numeration of these points in the manuscript is confused.

3. The priveledges of parlament.
1. Punishing out of parlament for things in.
2. Prohibiting votes in house on parlament.
3. Dissolving without the Consent of the house.
4. Not houlding parlaments according to lawe & statutes.

One thing left to Consider the pressing trayne Bands out of Counties.

Coppy of the Commission brought in.[1]

Mr. pymm.
That a member gave it him, Mr. Holborne.

Mr. Holborne.
Repayred to Lord Keeper the immediate warrant would first informe
the King. At 8 a clock went agayne, & tooke a Coppy by leave.

Commission read.[2]
Charles &c. which by act 25 H.8 recyting that the Convocation
assembled by writt, promise in *verbo sacerdotis* never promuldge Canons
without the kings assent soe enacted. That they should not without the
Kings assent. Noe Cannons be made contrary but be voyd. Ordered all
not preiudiciall should be inforcd. Know ye &c. Give & graunt
licence to William Canterbury & to Bishops, Arch deacons, &c. of
Canterbury. Shall & may propose agree &c alteration or newe
Cannons as they shall thinke fitt for the honor of the church & all
Eclesiasticall ministers in theyr distinct courtes. **p.65** & to debate
agree of such other poynts as wee shall deliver to, under hand or
signe manual to be treated of, Notwithstanding statutes or acts of
parlaments to the contrary. And all Cannons &c agreed on set downe
in writing & delivered to us to the end wee may allowe or disallowe the
Cannons, provided that the Cannons &c agreed on, be not contrary to
the Liturgy, Rubricks or 39 Articles or religion already established.
Or such as by letters pattents wee shall confirme.

Dockquett.
Lycence granted by this to Arch Bishops &c to alter or create new
Cannons or other matters in writing. To set in writing, to be allowed

---

[1]Aston's account has the fullest report of the debate over Charles' commission to
Convocation. See also *C.J.*, II, p.11; Cope, p.175.
[2]For the text of this commission, see *Foedera*, XX, pp.403-405. For further reading
about the relationship between Convocation and the Short Parliament, see *CSPD*,
1640, pp.24-25, 40; Esther Cope. 'The Short Parliament of 1640 and Convocation',
Journal of Ecclesiastical History (April, 1974).

provided not contrary as above nor any doctrine usuage & ceremonies already established.[1] 15th Aprill.[2]

Sir Iohn Hotham.
That when a Report made fit to be put to the question.

Mr. whythead.
He was at the clearke of the Crowne & saw such a Commission *verbatim, ergo* noe Innovations.

Mr. Hambden.
Noe answer. If newe Cannons why not to enquyre. The authority too large. The Cannons already caused suits. If newe more inconvenience. 2. Extent is to all persons whoe lawfully may be concernd in it. This cannot be otherwise understood then to bynd the layity. 3. The limitation. Things may be done lawfully. Recytes the Rubricks, Lyturgy, Articles, & all other things lawfully established by whom this may be interpreted dangerous. Motion that this may be consider[*ed*] as an Iuducement to innovation.

p.66 Mr. Controwler.
If extend noe further then the 3 former then it must result out of the practize.

Mr. pymm. Answer obiect.
Not propounded as innovation in it selfe but a cause to produce innovations. The former complayned of 3°Iacob.[3] Wee followe the steps of our Ancestors that they would not subiect them selves to the

---

[1]The King's Commission to Convocation: '... the said Canons, Orders, Ordinances, Constitutions, Matters, Causes and Things ... shall and may set down in such form as heretofore hath been accustomed, and the same so set down in Writing, to exhibit and deliver, or cause to be exhibited and delivered unto us, to the end, that We, upon mature Consideration by us to be taken thereupon, may allow, approve, confirm and ratify ... Provided always, that the said Canons ... consulted or agreed upon as aforesaid, be not contrary or repugnant to the Liturgy established, or the Rubricks in it, or the nine and thirty Articles, or Doctrine, Orders and Ceremonies of the Church of *England* already established. Provided also, and our express will, pleasure and commandment is, That the said Canons, Orders, Ordinances, Constitutions, Matters, Causes and Things, or any of them, so to be by force of these Presents considered, consulted or agreed upon, shall not be of any force, effect or validity in the Law, but only such and so many of them, and after such time, as We by our Letters Patents under our Great Seal of *England*, shall allow, approve and confirm the same, any thing before in these Presents contained to the contrary thereof in any wise notwithstanding' (*Foedera*, XX, pp.404–405).
[2]1640. See *CSPD*, 1640, p.40.
[3]For James' commission to Convocation, see D. Wilkins, *Magna Concilia* (London, 1737), IV, pp.378–79.

power of the cleargy more than the[ir?] Ancestors.[1] The cleargy
assembled by writt, should onely treat things agreed by parlament.
The Cannons made by them have bred great Confusion in church &
Kingdome.[2] More that it may be consulted on as a meanes to prevent
innovations.

Charles pryce.
Query whether the Gentelmen be prepared to treat upon the particulars.

Sir Ralph Hopton.
A weighty busines fit for consideration. Tis not to determine but to
Confer. Somthings as in way of right, Somthings as of Grace. Move
that it may be determined whether right questiond.

Mr. Ball.
Tis propounded that this Commission is occasion because innovation
when none. This nor in matter nor forme. Former Commission more
then one. Affirmed that the king can make noe cannons R. 2^{ds}time
different supremacy then in the pope, now tis in the King. 4°Iacob
twas resolved by all the Iudges that he might make Cannons. **p.67**
Moves that neither forme nor matter being newe, wee may leave it
out.

Lord Digby.
Mr. Ball on a ground. That this is noe innovation, but as inducing to
innovation.

Mr. Crewe.
Confirmes what Lord Digby sayes. They have power to make newe
Cannons. A good Commission may be ill executed & theerfore move
it to the question.

Put to the question. To be one head. 'I'.

Sir Philip[3]
Not thinke to have spoke to this. Notice taken of the same former
time. Say that was Complained of. & as hee conceived denied.

---

[1] For further reading on attempts by the Commons early in James' reign to exercise
influence over Convocation, see R. C. Munden, 'James I and "the growth of mutual
distrust": King, Commons, and Reform, 1603–1604', *Faction and Parliament*, ed. Kevin
Sharpe (Oxford, 1978), pp.66–68.

[2] I.e. the canons of Archbishop Bancroft of 1604. The Laudian canons of 1640 were
not issued until June. Cardwell, *Synodalia*, I, pp.245–415.

[3] Probably Sir Philip Mainwaring (Morpeth), though Sir Philip Parker (Suffolk) and
Sir Philip Musgrove (Westmoreland) also sat. *MofP*.

Mr. pymm.
Hee did not say soe.

Sir Philip.
First to understand what the inconveniences are that doe arize. 2^{d}not to goe to may bees.

Sir Hugh Chalmley.
Not intended that it should be presented as an innovation. It was resolved as an impediment, theerfore to vote it.

Mr. Harbert.
I will be strong in my owne sense till it be resolved, then I am over ruled. To the generall, not against it. But because innovations did fall theerfore fitt to complayne. Soe noe to determine them innovations but as Complained of.

Mr. Hambden.
Wee desire to make use of this by reazon of innovations complayned of.

Sir walter Earle.
The 2^{d}would resolve this.[1]

Sir Robert Harlowe.
2^{ds}his motion. House against it.

Mr. Crewe.
If you put it as you did you put both into one. Put to the question, hee cannot speake after the 'I'.

Mr. Lewckner.
That the woords were, before any such Commission. **p.68** Resolved on the question to make use of the Commission, by reazon of innovation Complayned of in matters of religion before the Commission.

2^{d}Head put to the question.

Mr. vaughan.
Because noe negative put againe.

The 2^{d}head voted. 3^{d}Head. Too generall.

---

[1] I.e. the second head. See above, **p.63**.

Mr. pymm.
Too many paticulars. Enough to prove some deprived, suspended, exommunicat. Divers for not reading the booke of the Lords day [i.e. *The Book of Sports*]. 60 in a diocesse conformable men put out.[1]

Mr. Treasurer.
By reazon of soe many particulars, put it is fitt to see them before the question.

Sir walter Earle.
2 petitions from bodyes of Counties theerfore noe need of proofe.

Mr. Contowler.
This can be but taken by implicite fayth without proofe.

Sir Ralph Hopton.
Put the question. Upon Complaynt & it may passe.

Mr. Speaker.
The woords are without warrant of lawe which wee have bin tender without sight of Records.

Put to the Question & resolved. Ordered.

4th Head: about popish tenents in printed bookes. That to be put Complayned of.

Sir william massam.
Produced a booke for prayer for the dead.

Mr. Controwler.
That popish tenents may be restrayned to tenents Contrary to our religion.

Sir Ralph Hopton.
That it may be it will satisfie many & can leave none unsatisfyed.

p.69 Put & resolved of by the Question.

---

[1]'O blessed Soveraigne, that thou didst but heare the severall cries and outcries of they people against these persecuting Prelates in many places, especially in our *Norwich* diocesse, where little Pope *Regulas* [Bishop Matthew Wren] hath played such Rex, that hee hath suspended above 60 [of] our sinceerest painfullest conformable Ministers, both from their Office and Benefice...' (William Prynne, *Newes from Ipswich* (Ipswich, 1636, p.4). See also R. W. Ketton-Cremer, *Norfolk in the Civil War* (London, 1969), p.69; William Lamont, *Marginal Prynne 1600–1669* (London, 1963), pp.38–39.

5 Head.That the Complaynt for restrayning Conformable ministers to preach in theyr owne chardge. Resolved by question.

Concerning propriety of our goods. 1st Head monopolies & restraint of trade.[1]

Mr. Treasurer.
I have noe interest in monopolie. But in this house wee goe against the order of house which wee have ever held to.

Mr. pymm.
That this house tender of monopolies & if particular monopolies complayned & voted, but now wee goe upon generalls, upon Complaynt from all parts of the Kingdome, & wee knowe Monopolies upon all. And present the Groanes.

Mr. Harbert.
Goe from the way resolved. If upon complaynt of particulars against the order of the house. 2^{d}ly a generall groaning of the kingdome upon all Commodityes which for the honor of the Kings Government I must say agayne, till it be decyded in the house cannot be presented.

Sir Iohn Hotham.
Wee suffer much in shipmoney, but let every man that is a house keeper consider what he suffers. Soape salt, fruitt, &c. Wee shall fynd much more cause then in ship money.

Mr. Hambden.
That it is not intended all Monopolies shalbe particularly treated with the Lords but the generall greivance may drawe us on particulars.

Put to the question & resolved
p.70 [blank]
p.71 [blank]
p.72 2 Head of goods, ship money.

Mr. pymm.
To distinguish whether wee complayne of the pressure of Legallity.

Sir Iohn Hotham.
If he held it Legell he would not Complayne.

---

[1]See above, **p.63.** The following report of the debate over the propriety of goods is unique to Aston's account.

Sir Iohn Strangwayes.
Wee must Complayne of the Legality for the money has bin soe well dispended, that wee have noe cause to Complayne ells.

Mr. Treasurer.
That wee should qualify it. Soe have noe dissenting voyce.

Mr. Glyn.
The woord Legallity ought not to be Complayned. Whyles a Iudgment in the Case, wee put a disadvantage upon our selves, because it is noe doubt a greivance in the execution.

Sir Hugh Chalmley.
Wee have ever waved touching the iudgment. This not in the nature of others. Nor bound in time, in limitt, therefore complayne of the illegality.

Mr. Iones.
Of the Legality not to proceed on it. Danger counter with a iudgment. When as great, complayned wee did not iudge it in 4° *Iacobi* in Bates his Case. 14 Argumentes in it. That the King of England in imposition *de iure* was equall in power to any King of England. They that did more did it by usurpasition. Another example: Liberty of person as deare as goods upon the *habeas corpus per mandatum domini Regis*. It was voted before wee proceeded. If upon the illegality noe man can argue under six weekes time.

p.73 Mr. maynard.
Would not add the woord generall, not that it would not enlarge the proceeding against this, but the want of the woord would restrayne the other.

Resolved that use be made of the Complaynts which have bin touching shipmoney. Voted: all agreed.

3ᵈHead. Use made of the complaynts of enlarging the Bounds of Forrests for some 100 yeares last past. Resolved by all.

4ᵗʰHead.
Imposition by way of military chardge in Coate & Conduct money, wages, Armes from owners, Horses & cartes by taxe. Query 'I'.

5ᵗʰHead. Use of complaynts in denying Iustice in courts of Westminster in poynt of property of goods. Resolved *per* question 'I'.

6[th]Head. Use to be made of the complaynts in Imprizonment for denying unlawfull monopolies. Ordered by question '(I)'.

Priveledges of parlament.
1. Punishing men out of parlament.

Mr. Speaker.
A man may [*sic*].

Mr. pymm.
1[st]poynt. The Lords equally interested with us. When they had question, in theyr iournalls made use of presidents of this house. The way of our ancestors Twas auntiently usuall. **p.74** President 5°H 4th all persons aresting or suing any member of the house of Commons should be imprizoned & fyned. 9°Henry 4 N°22° matters debated in this house not to be reported till debated & resolved. Commons requyre to depart with asmuch liberty as any our ancestors. 21 H 6. Thorps Case arested, conference of the Lords being in execution noe breach & another Speaker.

Mr. Glyn.
If wee did restrayne it to the Commons alone but query generall. Lords equally interested to confer, upon the generall not allowed, if murder or treazon may be questioned. For query of persons for things done in parlament to the breach of priveledge.

Mr. St. Iohn.
Not against priveledge to goe to the Lords.
1. All make but one parlament, E:3[d] divided. In case a member wee pray noe ayd wee may send a sergeant & release him, twas in the power. But this rests in iudgment, if wee goe to the Lords that Bynds both ioyning in iudgment.
Thorps Case in a recesse was arested and imprizoned. Went to the Lords & iudgment of both.
24. H 8, Farrar sitting was arested they sent resisted. All rise & went to the Lords. **p.75** 18 Iac. Twas ordered first to goe to the Lords. Our complaint being things done in another parlament, that dissolved wee can not doe any thing but goe to the Lords. Question: upon the Complaynt.

Sir william massam.
Resolved things done within the house.

Question Resolved *per* Question '(I)'.

2^dHead of Breach of priveledge by prohibiting votes in parlament. Resolved *per* Question 'I'.

3 Head. Dissolving without consent to be deserted.

Mr. pymm.
Desire that as our Auncestors may, by our petition pray noe dissolution till the subsidee come were setled.

Mr. Harbert.
Prayes it may be petitiond. But would have noe mention made of Complaynts against that being his undoubted prerogative.

Sir walter Earle.
2 statutes spoken of requyring frequent assembling parlaments when greivances happen.[1] If noe redresse this is a greivance.

Mr. Hambden.
Not whether a greivance, but whether fitt to goe the Lords on this, lay this aside for present.

Lay aside *per* question.

p.76 Last head about frequent parlaments.

Mr. Cowcher.
3 parlaments dissolved noe proffitt, universall discontent. Move to give him content.

Sir Ralph Hopton.
To confer with the Lords concerning those lawes for the frequent use of parlament.

Mr. Treasurer.
Glad to lay by this question. Many things in question which succeeding well will make him in love with us, take time & wee may then take it agayne.

Mr. St. Iohn.
Not the right of calling, but that of right it ought to be call'd once a yeare. 4 E 3, 36 E 3 by the petitions of the Countrey it hath bin held a greivance. The intermission of 11 yeares hath brought all this.

---

[1] 4 Edward III, c.14; 36 Edward III, c.10.

Mr. pellam.
In all ells noe Negatives, but of the consideration if wee see cause wee may put it another time.

Mr. Harbert.
The same right in this as in the other if wee say he may call when hee will, & say hee must call once a yeare, I cannot bee resolved how this can hang to gether. Seene the answer & considered, say bouldly upon the woords of it wee cannot pronounce this right. If the woords that sense 24 E 3 the practize unquestionably is when nothing was against it for 300 yeares practize. To resolve on a sudden that practize. Moove by petition to the king to call convenient time. But to dispute after many hundred yeares when a supply instantly pressing is requyred will not.

p.77 Sir Iohn Hotham.
The statute being infforce move to read it & then resolve.

All call to read it.

Sir Henry Mildmay.
Disadvantage at this time & relations. In all parlaments, observed when graspd soe much looze all. Pray all for frequent parlaments if a statute unrepealed, & if all statutes unrepealed should be put in execution. What inconveniences.

Mr. wynn.
The iudges never upon an ould statute resolve by the booke but resort to the Record.

Mr. pymm.
Of the same nature of the other & prayes to lay it by at this time. & thinke of a petition.

Resolved to be layd by.

The Lord Digby.
That it is left out to take the traynd Bands out of the County.

Mr. pryce.
Not out of the Kingdome. Layd by to a Committee.

The same Committee that drew up the heads to meete this afternoone at Court of wards to prepare matter on these heads.

Mr. Hambden.
Not to clog the busines with more heads. Power to the Committee to chardge the persons must undergoe this taske.

Sir Robert Harlowe.
The distribution of the parts. That the Treasurer & Secretary to be put in.

Mr. pymm.
to have power to send to the Tower for Records.

[Saturday, 25 April]

p. 78 April 25th

An act for naturalizing Iames Boore & Suzana a french woman his wife & mathewe his sonne. Shee of our religion & lived ever since 2 yeares.

Of old ordered to receive the Communion at St. margarets ells not to sit in the house. Now order all to receive *ut Supra* 3°May. Not to be admitted till he have received. Answer of his name and shire for which hee serves.

Godfrey.
To be observd the manner of receiving.

Dr. Farmero.
That course be taken about the oaths of Supremacy. A small Committee to examyne.

Mr. peard. A Report.
That petitions being preferd against Courts of Iustice, noe Councell to be gott unlesse they may be assigned. Ordered that they may assigne.

Mr. Speaker.
That Bills preferd in last parlament & some read may be brought in agayne. A Briefe read of ould Bills not finished against long imprizonment.

Mr. Glyn.
To have a care that the cleargy be not put in the Commission of peace. That soe much Spanish Wooll brought in as drawes downe the trade of this Kingdome.

Cradock.

Take heed least wee bring a greater Inconvenience. If wooll be transported into other parts, encrease theyr trade & mar ours.

Whithead.

It appears in all Countreyes that £3 is a losse every wheere which wilbe £300000 a year. Bill To be read on Tuesday.

p.79 Sir walter Earle.

To an account expected from the select Committee about the preparation of Account to the Lords. Not ready.[1]

Mr. pymm.

Debate to assigne the parts. Which without the resolution of the house noe power. Religion to him, he excuses himselfe from it. 2 poynts. Ordered that the Commission be a head brought in by reazon of Innovations without authority.[2] Confirmed those by this Commission theerfore prevent this. Agreed by the Committee an intimation to preserve the right of the subiect. Whether affirmatively or cautionarily, which might be preserved without diminution to be proposed & the long roabes to debate. 2ᵈ innovation by proceedings upon excommunication &c without lawe.[3] Both matter of greivance & matter of Cryme. Noe dischardge of duty &c, being criminall which may induce fynes & to be pronounced in parlament criminalls. Not to delay the Kings answeare. But to prosecute them in an ordinary way.

Mr. King.

Concerning the Commission. Good cause to make enquiry though not seene, cannons seene in convenience though they bynd not further then to the Comon lawe. Yet great interuption. Cannon. Minister to chooze a churchwarden.[4] How many suitts in Westminster. Overthrowen comonly but disturbing. Moove to hand the considered.

Mr. Speaker.

State of Pyms motion. Query to declare the right or to preserve it by

---

[1]I.e., an account of the list of grievances to be presented to the Lords, drawn up the previous day. See above, **pp.63–4, 77**.

[2]The commission to Convocation.

[3]See above, **pp.40, 68**.

[4]'All church-wardens or quest-men in every parish shall be chosen by the joint consent of the minister and the parishioners, if it may be; but if they cannot agree upon such a choice, then the minister chall choose one, and the parishioners another...' (Canon 89 of 1604 in Cardwell, *Synodalia*, I, p.296).

way of caution need noe debate. Time for Roabes to prepare debate.
Committee to proceed meanetime.

p.80 Sir Robert Harlowe.
Theere was noe doubt of reservation but upon what tearmes to reserve.
In the ould parlament warne of protestation to reservd.

Mr. waynsford.
Many forgot some to learne the old parlament way. I desire first to
know what that protestation shalbe first.

Mr. pymm. Answer.
It may be such a way as our ancestors have gone, wee may protest
not to be bound by any thing made by virtue of that Canon further
then it did bynd our Ancestors.

Dr. Farmero.
That it may not bynd further then this house, assents to them after
they are made.

Iudges from the Lords. Iones and Trevor.[1]
Message was that the King was yesterday with Lords that occasions
thence desire aspeedy conference with a Committee of this house in
the paynted chamber. Which is clearly a Committee of the whole
house except the speaker.

Mr. price to appoynt reporters.[2]
Mr. [sic] seconds the motion for Rushall a clearke to supply.[3]

Sir walter Earle.
Would first enquyre of the woorth of the man.

Mr. Speaker.
Noe man moves him as a clearke, the grant is in the King but tis in
the clearke.

Sir peeter Hammon.
No pericler, nor nomen clator to take notice of every woord that falls.

Resolved: not to take notice of any privat mans woords but to write
orders & reports.

---

[1]Justice Jones and Baron Trevor. *C.J.*, II, p.12; cf. *L.J.*, IV, p.68.
[2]Pym, St. John, Herbert, Grimston, Jones and Hampden were appointed reporters.
C.J., II, p.12.
[3]John Rushworth. *DNB*.

Ordered with many oppositions.

p.81 Then wee went all up to the paynted chamber wheere the Lords sit confusedly but move to sit as in the house.[1]

Lord Keeper.[2]
You the knights, Citizens & Burgesses. My Lords commanded mee to deliver the reazons & causes why they desire this Conference. His majestie did yesterday honor this house to come hither in person, & made many gratious expressions amongst the rest hee put them in mynd of what he had caused to be delivered before theyr Lordships the first day, & after in the banqueting house.[3] And that his majestie then gave his royall woord & assurance not to depart from one title of what had bin delivered but performe it really to the uttermost.[4] Then shewed the necessity of his present affayres would admitt noe possible delay. That at this time delay was as good as denyall. Then shewed us the Consequences. The present danger of the affayres & his owne honor in forreigne parts, which soe much conceived him to uphould, that it was deare as his life & did import him more to mayntayne it. Then since theere was a necessity of trust, hee us or wee him. In Civility & good manners, as well as in necessity, fitt to trust him. In conclusion begin with him or hee with you, there must be a totall trust in him in the execution. Wee differ now but in poynt of time wheerin wee must trust. Let us trust him in the beginning of the trust in part. Before the end hee must trust us withall. It is but a present supply without which all chardge is lost which is manifested to be £100000 a month. At least if wee delay wee make it impossible to recover it. My Lords commanded mee to put you in mynd what new intelligence did enforce dispatch, the necessity of the affayres **p.82** the urgency of the danger. Scotland begun already they had

[1] The following account of the Lord Keeper's speech was inserted into the manuscript at a later stage.

[2] There are two types of source for the conference with the Lords: accounts of the conference itself, and accounts of Edward Herbert's report of it to the Commons on 27 April. Aston's diary relates the Lord Keeper's speech as part of the conference itself. Aston merely noted, and did not describe, Herbert's report on the following Monday (see below, **p.87**). For other accounts of the conference, see Cope, pp.176–77, 201–202, 265–66; *L.J.*, IV, p.68. For Herbert's report of the speech on 27 April, see *C.J.*, II, pp.13–14; Cope, pp.231–32; Nalson, I, pp.333–35; Rushworth, III, pp.1144–46. For a discussion of the various accounts of Herbert's report, see Cope, pp.310–11.

[3] See above, **pp.1–3, 7–9.**

[4] The king reportedly said on the previous day: 'The House of Commons did seem to take into consideration My weighty Affairs; but they have in a Manner concluded the contrary; and, instead of preferring My Occasions in the first Place, they have held Consultation of Innovation of Religion, Property of Goods, and Privileges of Parliaments; and so have put the Cart before the Horse' (*L.J.*, IV, p.66).

pytch'd theyr tents at dunce & threatened Invasion of Northumberland; they have taken some of Sir william Brunkards troops.
Now there was noe iesting wee saw by letter they sought to put
themselves into the protection of a Foreigne. The necessity was such,
as twas not possible to transfer the trust from him to us, otherwise hee
would give us leave most willingly to goe on in our owne way. That
hee did onely requyre a present supply, & that then hee will suffer us
to goe on according to our desires. And then hee would give a gratious
eare to all our complaynts & releeve us fully as wee can in iustice
reazonably desire. That the Lords had taken notice of his woords,
that hee never held King for glorious as hee whoe commands a rich
& free people. That if hee did not secure us in our property of estates
hee could not account us a rich people nor consequently himselfe a
glorious King. Then tould us hee would willingly treat with us of
the three things exprest.[1] Religion, propriety of estate, liberty of
parliaments & would listen with a willing eare. Then hee made
protestation that the Religion of his heart & Conscience stood right
with the Religion of the church of England & as he had soe would hee
live & dye in it. And hee would be as ready to keepe out innovations in
the church as any man. That to that purpose hee would give a chardge
to his Bishopps to be very Carefull noe innovations should be suffred.
Then hee did agayne particularly mention shipmoney, that hee never
intended to make, never had made the least penny benefitt of it, but
to the contrary had layd **p.83** out many thousands for the preservation
of his Kingdome all his scope & ayme being our preservation in peace,
in plenty & in honor abroad, which could not otherwise have bin,
being all neighbour princes made soe great preparations. But let us
thinke of any other way to preserve the sea whatsoever, which by
reazon of the great preparation of other states doth soe much import
that without a mayntenance of a navy at sea it was impossible. And
let us under take to keepe the sea protect & defend him his majestie
would ioyne with us. That the Lords did Consider, they had not onely
the woord of a king, but as some of them observed of a gentlemen.
They would not distrust him. Yet they knew subsedies concerned the
Commons not them. They would not meddle with subsedyes but did
declyne it; yet being the good & safety of the Common wealth equally
concerned them being all but members of one body & equally concerned in the Common Safety, theyr interest in estate, themselves &
posterity, being equal, that they did take care all might goe well, &
wee must all ioyne to make this a happy parlament. That theerfore
theyr Lordships by vote declared they held it most fitt & necessary
the treaty of supply to proced all others, & therfore upon that desired

---

[1]The three heads of grievance compiled in the Commons on the previous day.

a Conference to let us know the reazons of theyr resolutions. And that this first considered, & this trust **p.84** Given, would be the greatest obligation to him, & the greatest tye of security to our selves that could be possible. That done they will then ioyne with us in all things concerning property of estate, liberty of parlament & propriety in all.

Lord privy Seale replyed; & wee are all ready to ioyne.

The Lords know you come but with eares to heare & not to confer they shalbe glad to treat when you have considered.

[1] **p.85 That the Lords did consider they had not onely the woord of a King but of a gentleman as some of them observed they would not him distrust more then of the greatest undutifulness toward him. Yet they knew subsedie concerned [?] us not them they would not meddle with subsedy. Did declyne it yet being the good & safety of the Common wealth equally concerned them being all but members one body & equall concernd in the Common safety, interest in estate, selves & take care all might goe well—a happy parlament. That theyr Lordships by vote declared they held it most necessary [word unclear] treaty of supply to proceed all others. & theerfore upon that desire a Conference to let us know the reazons & that this 1st considered & this [word unclear] would be trust the greatest obligation to him; & greatest tye of security to ourselves, that could be possible. That done they will then ioynd in all things concerning property of estate, liberty of persons, supply. To that I sayd Liberty of persons, I meant Liberty of parlament & property in all.

Lord privy Seale.
And wee are all ready to ioyne agayne. The Lords know you come but with eares to heare & not to Confer, they shalbe glad to treat when wee have considered.******

Sir Philip Manwaring.
The Committee being not ready & sending in a messenger to excuse them. Would have the same messenger goe for them. As against the priveledge of the house.

Sir Walter Earle.
That yt was noe novelty, hee had seene it 20 times. Yet gave way for Sir William Massam to call them.

Committee come in.

[1]The passage between the sets of ****** has been crossed out in the manuscript. It is probably Aston's rough copy of the Lord Keeper's speech at the conference.

Mr. Herbert.
We sent to excuse our selves by one of us. Care to doe it faythfully makes us requyerd here.

[Monday, 27 April]

p.86 April the 27th.

Rushall the clearke admitted.[1]

Mr. pymm.
Moves that ould orders may be looked up for that at the admission of wrights sonne an assistant.

An oath was given by the Speaker.

An act read touching the poynting of needles. Act brought in 60 yeares since now a trade. Mayntayne poore. Insafficiently done. Complaynes of an engine, preiudice of poore. Prayes an act not to use the engin payne of £5, none but prentizes.

Mr. Hambden.
A Bill concerning administrations, that the ordinary to dispose pious uses, upon a popish ground *pro animabus defuncti*. Inconvenience. Prayes that the Bill may be looked up.

Mr. Ball.
Remembers the Bill, that mr. Rowles had the Bill or has a Coppy to be sent to. Ordered.

Sir Thomas Barington.
That every man that has any may be ordered to bring them in. Ordered.

Mr. Cooke.
Moove for a Bill for reformation of abuses in Ecclesiasticall Courts. That many vexed with citations unto Ecclesiastical Courts that upon the creditt of a Summoner, excommunicate thereon to pay Fees & Compound. That the names of accuzors denyed to be knowne to be evailed that processe to be made according to act; E:6. That the processe to the statute, the cause contayned & the name of the party, & appeare by proctor & addition of his place. Coppy of the Libell for

---

[1] See above, **p.80**.

6d. if not prooved. Dismisse the cause **p.87** & damage. That if want matter force them on theyr owne oaths contrary to lawes humane & divine. Moves that none be forced. That excommunication is abuz'd. Unlesse in case of Blasphemy, adultery, incontinency & heresie; but [*sic*].[1]

Sir Guy palmes [*sic*].

A Bill concerning pressing souldgers.

Report calld for.

Mr. Jones.
Excuse for want of time. To propose notes.

Mr. Harbert made Report.

Sir walter Earle.
To the scope of this nothing, but to one passage reflect on the libertyes of this house. Liberty, parlament, subiect. 8. H: 4 due by lawe 2. H: 5. 11. H: 4. calld heart strings of the Common wealth. The Care of our anncestors to Keepe them inviolable amongst these one of weight as any. Liberty to order our owne busines as to the wisdome of the house shalbe thought fit especially greivance & supply. One passage trenches on that particular. Thoughe the Lords wave medling with subsedy yet they thinke it fitt & have voted it that the matter of supply be the first. The distinction for either as not satisfied. Trench on the liberty, soe for as fitt to Confer with the Lords to preserve the liberty.

p.88 Grymston.[2]
Hee would not dispute the vote of the Lords but rather wishd act of oblivion. To the argument itselfe for supply. These foundations, necessitated, without supply frustrate; consideration of delay as good as denyall. The Necessity came not from us, wee come being called not of ourselves without summons. If there be a necesity in that poynt not our faults, comanded sooner we'd had come. Wee had bin by my Lord Keeper Tould wee mighte to looke on the chariot & not guyde it, approach the arke but none but uzzas must lay hands on it.[3] Though wee are not to meddle with *arcana imperii* yet that any

---

[1] For a discussion of the procedure of the ecclesiastical courts, see Ralph Houlbrooke, *Church Courts and the People during the English Reformation 1520–1570* (Oxford, 1979), chaps. I, II.
[2] Harbottle Grimston the younger.
[3] 17 April.

blocks ly in our way wee may take them out that wee may guyd the chariot better. One was shipmoney. If that be Lawe & not over Ruled the King that sent for part might send for all. Confidence in the kings grace, & goodnes that he sent for noe more but wee may doubt heerafter the extent how dangerous. As it stands wee are not in Capacity to give. It was a rule in Philosophy *quod quis non habet dare non potest.* Let us be remitted into the condition of freemen & property restored, noe man but will adventure all his estat. I must needs rest heere with a heart full of sorrowe that I am forced to say I cannot give, I have not wheerwithall. Tis truth & I must say it, I cannot give.

p.89 Sir Beniamin Ruddiar.
Tis apparent the King is in necessity, & as certaine necessity is the woorst Counsellor. It were a good parlamentory woorke to remoove the great enemy necessity. I have said before The power of a king & the power of necessity will never be long in one hand. The matter whether trust the king it hath bin alleadged with ill successe, in the petition of right. The common law is soe civill that tis a maxime that the King can doe noe wroong. Woe & milstones to them that have wrought this diffidence betwixt the king & his people. The king hath promised fully to heare & releeve us. Let us doe that willingly which wee must doe whether wee will or noe. Our religion & liberties suffer. Wee that would not venture to save his religion let him perish. Wee that will not endeavour to releeve his greivances may he groane under affliction without releefe. My Care is to preserve parlaments. Whyles they stand Religion will flourish, wee shall roote out all oppression gradation: whoe takes care to any other purpose if not to preserve parlaments it is not to any purpose to care for any thing.

Mr. pymm.
The motion made for preservation of our priveledges was too great to dye too suddenly.[1] The Lord Keeper Records, if wee have noe counter Record it may rize up in iudgment. Often proposition hath bin to treat with us, noe hurt, but they propound to vote what they will treat, that supply should be first. This much to the breach of priveledge. **p.90** Moves not to passe it with silence, but wee must protest against it that it may be Record in future. That it was a vote Contrary to a resolution taken in this house, they vote supply first then the other parts. Soe there hath bin a direction of orders heere formerly & it was a great iniury & unfaythfulnes of this house, when wee had voted our way

[1] See above, **p.87**.

they by way of prevention vote before wee had mooved any thing. Vouched presidents. Protestation entred theere.

Mr. Glynn.
That he would not speake to the matter of supply but to 2ᵈfirst & mr. pymm. That some answer to the messadge which I will not say breakes the priveledge but treads on the heele of it very close. Perhaps if once it get the head in, the Body will followe. If the Lords had voted & moved it had bin a breach but they declare that they had resolved & voted, this comes as close as my be. The thing in debate digested into heads by us viz Religion, property & priveledge of parlament. Before wee present they vote the same thing by prevention. I had thought the doores opened to let out the members of this house, not the matters treated heere, which by the particulars they state as if present which is a bending of priveledge first: to the vote.

Mr. Controwler.
Nothing sayd with want of respect to this house. Tis desired by the king & the Lords intimated necessary to the Records, admitts them true. Never wise lawe maker tyed the bond soe fast that noe necessity might breake it. **p.91** Onely proper to divine majestie *uno intuitu* to foresee & prevent in conveniences. Hence infers in noe humane Constitutions, noe lawe soe strict but necessity may enlarge. Recytes Grymston that he could not give when the king demands. The king soe often inculcated that, there shalbe a propriety. Woorthy Consideration that the seas be preserved which by his revenue not possible. Noe cause but to proceed cheerfully to give supply as the Izrallites reckoned from egression out of Egypt. Soe that wee may make this a happy a parlament & reckon from hence all our happynes.

Sir Iohn Hotham.
A flatt breach of priveledges, if our money gone all our priveledges are broke. Looke in after ages. That it is first voted in the higher house wee shall goe to supply which is a Record, then wheer are our priveledges.

Mr. Holbourne.
Priveledges trenched on is a great Consequence. Subsedi naturally come from hence, they are the guyft of this house if arise from the motion from above then your thankes. If the Countrey not like it, wee the blame. 15°Eliz. this poynt in Question upon a message from the Lords upon a Record 9°H. 4 except When a difference how many, resolved meerly to belong to this house. In question: whether to Confer upon that poynt, resolved noe. They had a fayre answer that it was

a meanes of honor to stand upon the priveledge. **p.92** Rules have exceptions, necessity a mayne one. What necessity be never soe great. The Lords may tell us the danger; tis not enough to say they hould it fitt. Wee are united to a free Conference, if they declare first wee must submitt, then upon difference wee in cur a fresh danger if it had come in. 1st before vote heere it might passe with out exception, but when resolved they should goe in the first place if they take notice of the heads why not of the resolve. When to supply property I shall. Exception shall wee deny Conference what is to be expected. Answer. Hope wee had that wee may this proceeding onely to do our selves right, theyr Lordships will take it well to returne the same answer which was in the Queen's time that wee were tender to breake our priveledges. If Conference on a 3d thing denying Conference a Bar. But when wee must Confer on what they have resolved wee cannot but be at preiudice. Move that it may be on the 3 things.[1]

Mr. Ball.
Two questions, query: setle priveledges. 2d. Whether treat of supply. Noe way broke this of 15 E1 in question by his notes held 2 dayes debat, resolved contrary, that it was not against the priveledge. 50: E. 3. 8°time troublesome beging demand of ayd **p.93** & a Consultation of supply graunted. E.2. desired to Confer of supply with speed accordingly numero 27. Supply graunted 4. R. 2. 12°. The parlament begun 16 Nov. cause declared French Troubles The presse to treat next day. Considered accordingly, they did, desired a fuller declaration of reazon & ends—which done—the Lords & Commons debating subsedyes & 15 eers graunted. In the report the Lords are soe far from prescribing that did express it fit in the first place & resolve to treat with us. Our declaration was not to treat of supply last.

Mr. Iones.
In answer, The president was cyted rightly. He [Holborne] did not say twas a breach to Confer but twas a breach to direct the way. If a writt went to call a parlament to forreigne wars was express'd in the writt as trusted with the advice soe with the supply. But when wee resolve, to be preiudged precluded not to treat but upon condition, of supply first. Tis our greivance that they have chalked out our way, noe man can shewe a president to the Contrary.

Mr. Waller.[2]
Two reazons to inclyne us to protest against it. The breach of our priveldges, to which the King not inclyn'd. The 2d the trust wee

---

[1]I.e. the three heads.
[2]The remarks of the next seven MPs are unique to Aston's account.

should put upon his majestie of this prevented by the Lords theerfore
fit to consid[er].

p.94 Sir william massam.
Put it to the Question.

Mr. waynsford.
Woonders a question. Tis well sayd of Sir Benjamin [Rudyerd] Soe
to preserve parlaments as they may preserve us. If not in a parlamentary way wee are then upon a desperate one. The Lords had
not concluded us. Theyr opinion by way of advice not of authority.
Hee could not answeare the presidents of the long Roabe. Cannot
answeare, I wish I could.

Sir Robert Cooke.
The Kings business Suffer nothing more then by long debate. A
question whether broke, if resolved then how to releeve. The Lords
acknowledge the previledge in us[1] but when voted & then desire
Conference first resolve then Confer. They are land markes twixt King
& people. Twixt the 2 houses theere are bounds which must be
preserved by protestation. That done to goe on cheerfully.

Mr. Hyde.
That hee did not understand the woords wheere on the question.
Would heare them agayne.

Mr. Kerton.
That in all parlaments it hath bin stood on, theerfore a Committee
to consider & not enter suddenly on it.

Sir Robert Harlowe.
Sure the sooner to the resolution of this question, the sooner wee shall
satisfy the King.

p.95 Mr. St. Iohn.[2]
To asnweare presidents of H. 3d., by mr. Ball.[3] Presidents since H. 4.
Anno. 21. 22. To begin first was an absolute violation of priveledge. 9.
H. 4. same questioners thing carryed to the Kings eares, complayned
by the Commons That then concluded Lords alone, Commons alone,
& resolved noe thing spoke of to the Lords but voted resolved by the
speaker. Question then was whether there should be an encrease of

[1]See above, **p.83**.
[2]St. John's remarks are much fuller in Aston's account.
[3]See above, **p.92**.

Subsedies, which was delayed by the Commons; but, the question was
when onely to Confer, admitted. The Graunt is usually accepted with
the words *Gra mercy les Commons*, which have onely power of the graunt
of the Kingdome. A mayne violation in respect of time that they have
resolved supply in the first place which amounts to this that till this
done they will not treat with us. Which is the English of it. A gent
punished for saying parlaments were onely for subsedies made
incapable of ever bearing place in parlament. The Lords take notice
of the resolutions, hee not satisfied how this could come to passe.
Statute H: 4 that if any man informe his majestie hee should not heare
him. I feare the Lords have heard, what wee did & if Knew whoe
informed them I should not thinke him a fitt member to sit heere.
Protest against.

p.96 Sir Francis Seymor.
Wee are every day rendred more incapable then other to dispatch his
majesties busines. The Lords attribute much to theyr power or to our
weaknes to doe that at theyr desire which wee should not doe at his
majesties. Cheerfully & of our selves they should have the thankes of
it. Therefore to the question.

Mr. Speaker.
I thinke in my Conscience it had bin granted by this time had not
these interuptions bin.

Sir walter Earle put it that they had bin trenched upon.

Mr. Harbert.
If a question that it were & not to tell wheerin tis of such a latitude
as is undefinite. Wee need not despute it that supply does belong to
this house, tis yeilded by them [the Lords]. But as it has gone of later
times indisputable This sticks that what is said by the Lords is on 2
partes. One that it was delivered as matter of Conference. 2^d: the
reazons or inducements which weere necessity. I conceive given as an
advice by them, nothing can come from either house but by vote of
the house. As the sense of the house Consider it thus. As far as wee
conceive it a direction in quantity or circumstance in giving it would
be an entrenchment but they say they would not meddle with matter
of subsedy. If that house weighing well the Condition of the present
state in relation to religion, to propriety of goods, whether they may
not by theyr knowledge a particular wheerof instance they gave. **p.97**
If many if all togather knowing what that wee know not doe but offer
this as theyr advice that beleave it most necessary to goe on first.

Whether this may not be taken into Consideration as noe breach of priveledge requiring a necessity being members of the same body & then make a question.[1]

Sir Miles Fleetwood.
Extreame sorrowe as even every day more into streights. He did beleeve ould parlament men had a free hearts as ever men had: before wee proceed wee must be enabled. The priveledge are broke directing us the way, wee would doe it clearly & ingratiate with the king. Vote whether they have done us wrong & consider the way.

Mr. Controwler.[2]
Hee had rather carry out a cleare Conscience & leave a suspected, they carry away a suspecte one & leave a cleare one. The Lords did not direct us any thing.

Mr. pymm.
Too the orders of the house. I was Loath to interupt the gentleman but twas against the orders having spoke to the matter. Move noe man that has spoke may spoke [sic] agayne.

Mr. vaughan.
Question once spoke not to be layd aside. To vote generally before reduc'd improper reason. What voted by the Lords as a hygh breach: that wee cannot proceed in any thing for the Common wealth till that be stated. **p.98** Whyle they have voted it is necessary noe receding. Then followes that wee can have neither greivance reduced nor Iustice till Supply, theerfore prayes it may be read agayne or a way taken.

Mr. Treasurer.
Confesse the streights was not at Conference. That the woords may be read agayne, or a Committee.

Mr. Hollis.
Wee are all fellowe members, of one Body, that which keepes us entyre, gives us life is our priveledges. Wee represent the whole Commonwealh. If the Lords had prescribed us the graunt to come in the first or last place. It had bin a breach of priveledge.

[1] See above, **pp.81–83**.
[2] The remainder of the report of this day which follows, contains the speeches of individual MPs which are almost exclusive to Aston's diary.

Mr. Pryce.
Query to name a Select Committee.

Sir Iohn Hotham.
Twas already fully debated to put it to the question.

Sir Henry mildmay.
If a wound given, happy hee that can apply a remedy. To make it
perfect for a question.

Sir Robert Crane.
That the woords may be read agayne.

Mr. Harberts reads the woords agayne.

Sir peeter Hammon.
If wee declyne the question wee declyne our owne right. As many as
are of opinion that the priveledges of this house in the last Conference
with the Lords are broken say 'I'. Resolved upon the question.

Sir Peeter Hammon.
Would have Committee of the whole house.

p.99 Mr. Glynn.
Not ready till a Committee of the whole house or a Select Committee
have voted the particular.

Sir Iohn Culpepper.
That it cannot stand with the honor of the house to refer that to a
Committee to resolve of the particular which wee have voted in the
generall, least if there should be a difference in opinions wee might
be preiudiced.

Mr. Sergeant wyld.
The like accident 18°debated & resolved that they ought not take the
least intimation from the Lords.

Mr. peard.
Both the proposing & voting are both breaches. The proposing is an
assaulting, the voting a wounding of our priveledge.

Mr. vaughan.
That stating generalls & voting them first & then being to seeke
particulars is very preiudiciall. Theerfore the woords to be Read
againe & drawne to a question.

Mr. Cooke.
The woords particularly set downe in the question.

Sir Benjamin Rudyar.
That pronouncing the woords was generall. Theerfore the woords to
be set downe.

Sir Raloph Hopton.
The particulars 2 positive, the proposition, the voting, are absolutely
breach of priveledge. The other woords are but of inference & would
not have them voted but onely the positive woords.

p.100 Mr. Glynn.
To explane a mistake. That fit the house into a Committee, for that
every man may freely speake to the particulars.

Mr. Hambden.
Some difference amongst us how to resolve if, noe need of Committee.
That the Lords medling with the supply & voting it that was a breach.
2^d: that confering with us & prescribing us by that advice what shalbe
first, are both breaches.

Mr. pymm.
The same ells exception that voting perhaps had bin none.

Lord Digby.
If I miscollect not the sense of the house it is in these then 2 questions:
1. Whether the Lords intermedling in subsidy & voting it in theyr
house were a breach of priveledge.
2. Query whether in Conference with us prescribing & chalking the
way was not a breach of priveledge.

Mr. Hollis.
If wee goe noe further wee have done little. Wee have but drawne a
Lead Rule it may be appyled to any thing: therfor complyes.

Mr. Harbert.
Hee could not give his consent to those questions: the woords 'chalking
out the way' were lyable to exception.

Sir T[*homas*] A:[*ston*].
That the question should not be divided which would not hould in it
selfe in part to be breach of priveldge. For them to vote in theyr house
& not declare to us wee could take noe notice of it. To offer advice

without voting or prescribing could be noe breach neither. Theerfore
putting all into one question: whether the Lords declaring that they
had voted the matter of supply to be in the first place. Would determine the question.

p.101 Question put & resolved.

Sir Iohn Hotham.
Doubts whether our protestation will be of authority sufficient.
Without wee goe to the Lords, wee being noe house of Record.

Mr. Hollis.
Moves that a Committee shall prepare the matter, for a Conference
with the Lords.

Mr. Kerton.
Not too many of the Committee breed confusion. The same Committee that made the report & six more added.

Sir walter Earle.
That it hath bin a Constant Rule of this house that any man that
hath spoke against a Bill or a Committee shall not be of the Committee
for that Bill or busines.

Mr. Harbert.
Concerned him selfe & he hold it fit to be kept A fundamental order.
That noe man that was against a Busines should be of the Committee
for it & pr [*sic*]. Therefore constant order any man that speekes against
a Bill or a Committee should be left out & prayes he may be excusd.

Mr. Hambden.
Noe Rule without an exception. Instances a matter concerning the
Citty wheerin they that spoke against it were in & in the discusse [*sic*]
having reference to the report would have him in.

Sir walter Earle.
Time & place for the Select Committee 2 a clock in the afternoone.

Sir william massam.
That the 3 heads shalbe prepared & reported to morrowe morning
for matter of Conference with the Lords.

[Tuesday, 28 April]

p.102 28th Tuesday.

A Bill. For elections. Recytes former elections & the acts. That the mayors may give oath to discover true electors. Noe promises of Rewards, meate, drinck or money.

Mr. Rigby.
To throw it out.

Mr. Alestree.
To be committed & reformed.

Mr. Lenthall.
Move that it may be retained.

Mr. Iones. Report.
Election of Beareonson [Berralston, Devon]. Mr. Stroud, Mr. Harris,[1] Sir Amias Meredeth.[2] The precept 6th. 26 appeare. That then Mr. Stroud, Sir Nicholas Slaning[3] & That Mr. Stroud should be burgesse. Execution put off till 27 [of March]. That he to be Burgesse if either were knights. Mr. Wise was made for Devon.[4] 27 [of March]. Mr. Harris, &c. All 3 returned. Sir Amias, 12. Mr. Stroud, 6. Harris, 18. Query, whether an election first day.
2 whether with a condition,
3 whether an election the last.
Resolved that on condition subj[ect] to an election voyd if upon a precedent *de facto* performed. Maior part agree conditions preced or subsidy. Voyd, cause elections ought to be free. That if 1st day all 3 standing in Case but on agreement, and extend to his election then his voyd. But if cleare the first day then condition voyd. Found yt noe condition annexed in the same **p.103** election, but before & after it was treated amongst the parties soe voted & resolved. Except, that he was chosen 2ᵈtime. 3ᵈthing that his Indentures returned after which makes nothing.

Mr. Harris admitted upon the question.

---

[1]John Harris (Beeralston). Keeler, p.204; *MofP.* Cf. 'Mr. *Harding*' (*C.J.*, II, p.14).
[2]Sir Amias Meredith failed to gain a seat. See below, **p.204**; *C.J.*, II, p.14; *Reports and Transactions of the Devonshire Association* (vol.XLI, 1909), p.158.
[3]Sir Nicholas Slanning (Plympton Earl). Keeler, pp.339–40; *DNB*.
[4]See below, **p.203**.

Mr. Tomkins.
That it was but a Communication.

Mr. Baber.
That the ceremonies were performed.

Mr. peard.
It did cleerly appeare the election absolute & the condition after.[1]

Question. Resolved upon the Question & admitted. Order that the
3[d] Indenture be withdrawne.

Mr. waynsford.
Move that however this resolved in mr. strouds case this house not to
favour conditionall elections.

Iones. Borrough of Bedwin.[2]
Election to the Burgesses, Bayliffe & port Reave & such as had bin
Bayliffes. Said that the election was to all that paid Scott & lot. 3
chozen, one 52, one 31, another 21.[3] Appeares by Returnes that all
elections had bin made by recommendations. Committee not resolved
to whom belonged. Mr. Harding, mr. Seymor stand.[4] Ob:[ject] that
returne made by a precept to be done the 24th of march, which was
done the 30th. Resolved the sheriffe not to limitt a time.[5]

p.104 Sir Iohn Davers.[6]
Not oppose report. Ob:[ject] That wittnesses not fitt ot be Complay-
ners. But mr. Francklyn chardged for undue Carriage. Suggestion
mayntayned. Expected penalty. Noe man delivered any thing but the
man himselfe. He delivered that one had 50 voyces, & in the whole
borough: not above 32. 22 gave voyce for Cordware at Sir Iohn's
recommendation.[7] Move the election may stand, but that 20 Super-
numerary may not preiudice the freedome of the Borrough. 2dly for

---

[1]See below, **pp.205–206;** above, **p.103.**

[2]Jones continues to report from the Committee of Privileges on the disputed election
at Great Bedwin, Wiltshire. See *C.J.*, II, pp.3, 14–15; and especially the committee
report of 16 April (below).

[3]See below, **pp.198–200.**

[4]Richard Harding (Great Bedwin); Keeler, pp.202–203. Charles Seymor (Great
Bedwin); *MofP*; *Wiltshire Archaeological and Natural History Magazine* (vol.VI, 1860),
p.300. Cf. 'Mr. *Sayer*' (*C.J.*, II, p.15). See below, **p.199.**

[5]For further information about this disputed election, see Hirst, p.78; Keeler, p.70,
202; *VCH Wilts.*, V, p.135.

[6]See Danvers's remarks in the committee meeting on 16 April (below).

[7]Cf. 'cordwell, 21 [*votes*]' (below, **pp.199–200**).

misdemeanor. Considered mr. Francklin had committed misdemeanor may be proceeded upon in parlament or after.

Mr. Iones.
Burough of Mounmouth. Ordered that every man may make his election in x days. He is returned for mounmouth[1]

p.105 Mr. St. Iohn.[2]
The Committee reduced into writing theyr resolution.[3] *Die luna* 27 April, stile an addresse to the Lords.
1. That a message to the Lords for Conference concerning the trenching on the preveledges of the Commons house upon theyr acknowledgement that matters of subsedy belong to this house, & declyned it. Noe presidents mayntaine it. But theyre Lordships have advised both of matter & manner of supply before it was moved to them.[4] Voted it necessary & fitt to proceed. Any other matter what soever desire Confer[ence] to know theyr reazons. Then to ioyne in the 3 heads. The Course offred that theyr Lordships be desired in theyr wisdome fynd out some way of reparations for present, prevention for future. Committee induced to conceve the Commons on debate 3 heads were to proceed supply.[5] That the Lords Conceived the 3 heads on which notice the Commons resolved to treat. Desire to present in those woords that in case they have taken the 3 heads were treated. Avoyd inconvenience in time to come they desird heerafter take noe notice till they shall declare it, which they shall all times observe to the Lordships, as desirous to preserve the priveledges of either house. Conceiving the contrary not to stand with the priveledges of either house.

p.106 Mr. Hambden.
Observe a generall silence, takes it a Consent if soe. Next to chooze a Committee, to present this to the Lords. Moves that mr. pymm may doe it.

[1]William Watkins sat for Monmouth Borough. *MofP*; Keeler, pp.56, 381; Gruenfelder, *Influence*, p.188. It is possible that this entry refers to 'Jones' Double Return' (see *C.J.*, II, p.15).
[2]The remainder of Aston's account of this day up to Pym's speech in the Painted Chamber is by far the most detailed.
[3]I.e., the report of the committee authorised on 27 April to prepare another conference with Lords. The Commons were concerned with the Lord Keeper's speech of 25 April in which he urged, on behalf of the upper house, that supply should be made to the king before any redress of grievances. Many members of the Commons considered the Keeper's action a breach of the privilege of the lower house. See above, **pp.81–84, 87–101**; below, **pp.109–114**.
[4]See below, **p.83**.
[5]See above, **pp.63–77, 101**.

Mr. pymm.
That it may be mr. Hambden.

Sir Iohn wray.
One move, the other assist.

Sir Iohn Culpeper.
That one woord, confessed, which is conceived upon accusation, acknowledged is enough.

Sir Ralph Hopton.
Being it must be a Record it were fit to be cleere. Agrees with Sir Iohn acknowledge 2 woords. Ells That theyr Lordships have medled. Better dealt. Wee have cause to cause, [*sic*] to suspect &, conceive. The woord medled was theyr owne woord. The word Confessed altered to admitted.[1]

Mr. pryce.
All the business of the Common wealth depends upon this move, an act of oblivion, not to divid the Lords and us.

Sir Iohn Hotham.
Not to the motion, but to the busines. Move that mr. Solicitor may doe it.

Mr. Solicitor.
Never was nor shalbe unwilling to serve the house. Did not attend the Committee. Did not heare it read. Continue order that the best acquaynted may serve. I did not heare it read I doe not understand it. Move that mr. pymm & mr. Hambden.

Mr. pymm.
I hope for all lawfull favours. Desire excuse, did not heare it. Rather suffer for his disabilities then his disobedience. **p.107** Desires to withdrawe halfe an howre & will returne.

Sir william massam.
Not resolved that this shalbe the addresse. Resolved that it shall by the Question.

[1]See above, **p.83**.

Speaker.
Report made. The King expects an account. Put us in mynd of it.

Sir walter Earle.
Resolved that a message goe to the Lords to crave a Conference. By that time the gentleman [Pym] will returne.

Mr. Treasurer.
That if possible goe to the Lords and gett of this business.

Mr. Treasurer moved to goe to the Lords to crave the Conference.

Mr. Solicitor.
To put this in the way, as an honorable person to goe, to intimate somewhat of the nature. That it may be to Confer concerning som-thing that fell in the late Conference[1] touching the priveledge of parlament.

Sir Thomas Berrington.
Read that offred by the Committee it will satisfie the house.

Mr. Hollis.
More modest to limitt it to woords of this house.

Sir walter Earle.
To move if they please a Committee of both houses. That it is unfitt to goe till the gentleman come back, the Lords may perhaps send to come presently & then wee are not ready.

p.108 The Lords.
Answer that they will meete us with a Committee of both houses presently as wee desire.

**[2] Mr. pymm.
My Lords I am Comanded &c to represent the desire & care that house alwayes had & now have to preserve such union and cor-respondence between the two houses of parlament as may not onley preserve [?] the respect & unity & priveledges of both house but be of expedition to dispatch the affayres of the Kingdome according to his majesties expectation. The Lords [*word unclear*] that there are some priveledges of this house not onely Ceremoniall & of forme, but

---

[1]On 25 April.
[2]**P.108,** between the ******, is a rough copy of Pym's speech that has been crossed out in the manuscript. **Pp.109–112** have been inserted into the diary.

alsoe substantiall, fundamentall & essentiall to the foundations & subsistence of the houses which enable them to subsist with that power, & honor they have. They hope your Lordships will consider that as its the highest Court of Iustice in this Kingdome it hath bin the care of both houses & ever deare to them to preserve the priveledges of both houses. Both such as are generalls to both & peculiar to each house. Now being all members of one great body, if Confusion fall in the body of the parlament that which is the fountayne from whence should flow all good to the Kingdome if there be disaccord betwixt the members of one body insteed of a fountaine of good followes Confusion, & soe can come noe good. I am commanded by the house to this service, Toe certify your Lordships that they took notice your Lordships did admitt that it was onely proper to this house matters of subsedie & supply & theyr grants to begin there, which they need not goe about to prove, since your Lordships acknowledge it in your Conference. But they Conceive your Lordships in the pursuit vary even in part—not in your intentions to preiudice the libertyes of the house. In your last Conference your Lordships were pleased to tell us the matter of danger which was the nature of that Conference **

p.109 Mr. Treasurer.
Delivers the message to the Lords that they desired to Confer with them. They returne answeare that they will meete us with a committee of both houses presently as wee desire.

Mr. pymm.
Being come with all the Committee into the paynted chamber. Begins: My Lords, I am Commanded by the knights, Citizens & Burgesses of this house of Commons to represent to your Lordships the desire & care that house alwayes had & now have to preserve such union & Correspondence betweene the two houses of parlament, as may not onely preserve all fayre respects & unity betwixt them, & to keepe inviolate the priveledges of both houses, but be of expedition to dispatch the affayres of the Kingdome according to his Majesties expectation. Your Lordships know that there are some priveledges of this house not onely ceremonial & of forme, but alsoe substantiall, fundamentall & essentiall to the foundations of both the houses, which enable them to subsist with that power & honor they have. They hope your Lordships will consider it as it is the Highest Court of Iustice in this kingdome it hath bin the care of both houses & they have bin ever deare to them to preserve the priveldges of both houses aswell such as are generall to both, as peculiar to each house. Now being all members of one great body, if Confusion fall in the body of the parlament, that which is the fountayne from whence should flow all

good to the kingdome, & that there be discord betwixt the members of that body insteed of a fountayne of good must needs followe **p.110** Confusion, & soe can come noe good. My Lords, I am Commanded by the house to this service And am to Certifie your Lordships that they tooke speciall notice that your Lordships had observed, the matter of subsedie & supply did onely & properly belong to this house & begun there, which they need not goe about to prove. Since your Lordships did in your Conference acknowledge the same. But they conceive that your Lordships did afterwards vary from that rule in part, not in your intentions to the preiudice of the libertyes of this house. For that your Lordships had bin pleased to impart unto us by way of advice the matter of danger which was the motive of that Conference, & your Lordships did then admitt not to meddle with graunting of subsedies, as a right due to us to flowe from us. Yet in persuit heerof your Lordships did impart other matters, & in discussion of those the house did Conceive your Lordships went beyond those Bounds, in that your Lordships did declare you had voted it necessary & fit that the matter of supply should have precedence, & that being done your Lordships would ioyne with us in Conference of the other poynts: of innovations in matter of religion, in that Concerning the propriety of our estates & **p.111** & [*sic*] priveledges of parlament. Now my Lordships, they [the Commons] conceive that if it were not proper for your Lordships to meddle with subsedies, to vote it in your house comes soe neere it they know not how to distinguish. To give advice is of another nature, but to vote that as first cannot be but to seeme to preclude & prescribe them the way, & this Concernes them not in theyr being onely but in theyr well being, as preiudiciall to the greatest & most essentiall of all theyr libertyes. They know your Lordships in your wisdome will fynd out a way how to repayre this that it may not heerafter rise up in evidence or remayne upon Record agaynst them. I am likewise further to signifie that they conceive that by enumeration of the three heads wheerin your Lordships are willing to ioyne with them, that your Lordships have taken notice of some things done in that house, without any motion from them to your Lordships, which is the Highest of theyr priveledges & was in former parlaments established in great Solemnity & called the great indempuity [indemnity] of the Commons.[1] Theerfore they pray that heerafter **p.112** your Lordships will take noe notice of what is or shalbe done there till they represent it to your Lordships, assuring your Lordships they wilbe tender in theyr Consultations to advize of nothing but what shall tend to the preservation of religion, the honor

---

[1]See Glynne's remarks on 27 April (above, **p.90**).

of the King, the good & safety of the kingdome, & the iust preservation of the priveledges of both houses.

p.113 **[1] Your Lordships did admitt not to meddle with graunting of subsedies as a right due to us to flowe from us yet in pursuit you did impart other matters, & in discusion of those the house did conceive went beyond thouse bounds. In that your Lordships did declare you had voted it necessary & fitt that the matter of supply should have precedence & that being done your Lordships would ioyne with us in Conference of the heads: innovations in matters of religion, propriety of estate & priveledges of parlament. If it were not proper to meddle with subsedies then to give a vote, is to meddle. To give advice is of another nature but to seeme, preclude & prescribe them the way Concernes them not in being but well being, as pre-iudicall to the greates & most essential of all theyr Libertyes. They know your Lordships in wisdome will fynd out a way how to repayre this that it may not heer after rise up in evidence of remayne upon Record against them. I am likewise further to signifie that they Conceive that by enumeration of the 3 heads wheerin your Lordships are willing to ioyne with them, that your Lordships have taken notice of some thing done in that house which is the Highest of theyr priveledges & was established in great solemnity & caled the great imdempuity of the commons. Theerfore they pray that heerafter your Lordships will take noe notice of what there is done, till they represent it assuring to your Lordships that they wilbe tender in theyr con-sultations to advize of nothing but what shall tend to the preservation of religion, the honor of the King, the good & safety the Kingdome &c the iust preservation of the priveledges of both houses.******

p.114 Mr. pymm. [*sic*]

Sir walter Earle.
That the Committee did meete, did what possible in that time. Saturday Conference of the Lords did intervene, part of the Committee of this latter, soe that they could not prepare it. This afternoones woorke will perfect it.

Mr. Hambden.
2d the motion entring the paper.[2] And that the Report be entered made by mr. Harbert.[3]

---

[1] **P.113,** between the set of ******, is a rough copy of Pym's speech that has been crossed out in the manuscript.
[2] I.e. Pym's speech.
[3] I.e. Herbert's report of the Lord Keeper's speech of 25 April.

[Wednesday, 29 April]

April 29th.

Mr. Speaker.
A suit brought against Sir peeter Temple by the Lord Baltinglasse.
Move for stay of it.

Mr. vassall.
Moves a longer time & addition to the Committee for the surveigh of
the account of the subsedies graunted. 3 Subsidies, 3: 15ths 21 Iacob.

Mr. waynsford.
Rather wanted a Solicitor noe one attended.

Mr. Kerton.
This house full of business not fit to give them a dischardge.

Mr. Cage.
This motion not a stranger, order the Committee to Consider of it.

2 Bills brought in according.

Mr. vassall.
A briefe of 7 or 8000 popish bookes taken notice of at the Custom by
one Iones. Delivered by the Lord Canterburyes order to Iones. Register of the Hygh Commission office. William Iones, Adrian tent [sic].

p.115 Sir Gilbert Gerrard.
That 15 Jesuitts taken by one Newton, a messenger, to [sic] & are
released with out knowledge or account why.

Vassall.
That the bookes [sic].

Waynsford.
You expect a speedy returne of theyr labours: it does not appeare but
there hath bin care for suppressing them. An order for them to attend
the Committee.

A Bill.
To enlarge the Liberty of preaching By want of Competent mayntenance, men cyted for going to other Churches when they have none
at theyr owne. That they may not.

3 Bills Concerning administrations read.

1. An act to imploy Commutation money to pious uses. Payne of loozing ten times as much to repayre of Bridges, wages or other good uses by the Iustices in Sessions. Account, kept in a Register booke on payne of £20.

2d. Bill. Concerning graunting of Administration to those that belong not. If any dye intestate or will executors, refuzing ordinary, not graunt within x dayes. If voyd, Then to husband or wife, if refuze, to the eldest requyring or not refuzing. If then to the other sonnes. If noe sonnes or refuz'd, Then to the daughters successively. If without issue, or refuzd, then to the next of kin. **p.116** Then to the next heyre at Common lawe. Soe successively to all. If none of these, Then to the Creditors most meete. Then to the Legatees of the intestate, provided ordinary to take Bonds & graunt warrants upon graunting.

3d. Bill. Abuse Compelling executors by the ordinary to dispose the goods. Noe executor compelled by any ecclesiasticall Court. But informe, if he have noe issue, then the executrix the sole benefitt. If children & wife dower then child 2 parts. If noe dower the children unadvanced shed 1/2, they the other. If noe wife, children. If none, his brothers, if noe brothers, sisters. If none to the executor or administor, provided noe custome of towne or Citty to be broke. As if this act had not bin.

Sir Guy palmes.
A Course to bring in Breifes with these Bills.

An act for Reformation of elections.
That noe peere nor privy Counsellor shall send any letters or messages for knights. Punished by fyne or imprizonement. Iustices shall enrowle the letter of Sessions. £20 forfeited, any Concealing shalbe indited. That noe man have voyce that hath not £X. **p.117** Noe Burrough, but such as are bodyes politick or incorporate.

Ordered to be throwne out.

Sir Iohn Hotham.
Never lesse cause to Complayne of Lords letters. Why should wee restrayne the liberty of Free elections.

Mr. Speaker.
That it may be referd to the Committee of priveledges to Consider of some fitt Bill by a subcommittee & refer to the house.

Ordered accordingly.

Mr. Tompkins.
Calls for a Bill to exempt Salop, woster, Hereford, Gloster from the Iurisdiction of the Marches. Bill against tomorrowe.[1]

Report. Sir walter Earle.[2]
Apologie that one day of Interuption, cast us further back then two recover. To prepare the Conference. With the Lords in the 3 heads. 1st place that 3 members be made choyce of eich one 3 heads. Mr. pymm: for Religion & introduction for all. Mr. St. Iohn: propriety of goods. Mr. Holbourne: priveledge, parlament. 1st fitt that a saving be in the Commission that the Cannons not binding but by parlament. This by protestation.
2. [1.] Complaynts but of innovations in generall by moving Communion Tables. [2.] Setting up Crosses, Images & Crucifixes. [3.] Refuzing to administer but at the Rayles [and] excommunicating. 4. Making Articles at visitations without warrant. **p.118** 2d. [5.] Suspending ministers without warrant. Instance in those that read not the booke for pastimes. Observed whether a Crime. [6.] As for printing, preaching, &c some not yet perfect. [8.] Restrayning Conformable ministers in theyr owne chardges in Bath & wells, Lincolne &c.
2. Propriety of goods.[3] 1st mayne shipmoney. Legality voted in this house. First if wee hould it illegall why complayne? 2. Enlarging Bounds of Forrest. 3. Monopolies, Salt, Soape &c. 4. Restraint of Trade. 5. Military matters, takng away the traine Bands. Lincolnshire, essex, middlesex, & other taxes now sitting [?] parlament To have this voted whether legall or not. Courts of Iustice. Instances of mr. vassalls, Lord viscount Say, Chambers & others. Unwarratanble [sic] taxes. Instances to be given.
3. Breach of Liberty in parlament:[4] Instances mr. Selden, mr. Holles, Sir peeter hammon, mr. stroud. Resolved that the matter of fact shalbe referred to that which was voted.

p.119 A lettere to mr. upton from mathewes mayor of [sic, but most likely Dartmouth].[5] Lords letteres for 2000 souldyers. Warrants for £3000.

---

[1]See below, **p.130**.
[2]Report of the committee preparing a conference with the Lords on the three heads of grievances. See above, **pp.63–77**.
[3]Aston's account of the report concerning the second head is the fullest. See above, **pp.69–73**.
[4]Other sources do not include any mention of the third head on 29 April. See above, **pp.73–77**.
[5]Keeler, p.270.

Sir Thomas Barrington.
To begin as they were reported & to come to this in due time.

Mr. St. Iohn.
Desire to be excus'd in the whole if not many particulars. Desires an addition of one to assist him.

Mr. pymm.
Till the house resolved the parts not seazonable this motion.

Mr. Speaker.
It usuall that the Speaker going [?] upon any busines there was a protestation that nothing from him should preiudice the right of the Commons.

Question: That in this Conference with the Lords there shalbe a protestation for saving the right of the Commons, not to be preiudiced or commanded by any Cannons that are or shall be made by any Commission graunted.

Mr. vaughan.
Caused the words subiect restrayned to Commons.

Mr. Hambden.
That the Commission be named ellse it will not be knowned what it was was [sic] meant.

Coucher.
Moves to enter & bring it to good effect & looze noe time. Cryed downe.

Mr. Hyde.
That it is not Contrary to the Rubrick that the Communion Table stand alter wise.

Lord Falkland.
To Read the Rubrick & then resolve.
Question: whether The removing the Comunion Table Contrary to the Rubrick in the question.[1]

---

[1] 'The Table having at the Communion time a fair white linen cloth upon it, shall stand in the body of the Church, or in the Chancel, where Morning prayer and Evening prayer be appointed to be said' (*BCP*, 1559, p.248).

p.120 Sir Robert Harlowe.
The forme of religion, trenches upon religion. All our ancestors suffred for these woords *Hoc est Corpus meum*, & are not wee brought almost to Idolatry, in bowing to that.

Mr. Rowse.
Produces Dr. Coppinger: That wee ought to doe all reverence to the most Holy Altar wheere is always the reall presence of the Body of Christ.

Sir william massam.
A Booke to that purpose.[1]

Sir [Edmund] Mounford.
A Sermon at Norwich. Somthings by practize something by precept. Bowing to the Altar taught by example.[2]

Sir Iohn wray.
That the Lord of Canterbury set out in a booke that at the Altar is alwayes *Hoc est Corpus meum*, at the pulpitt, *verbum Domini*.[3]

Lord Falcand.
Divide them other wayes, some will give theyr votes to one, will not give theyr vote to the other.

Dr. Eden.
If it be but particular act noe act of the universitie, to erect Crosses or Contrary to the Rubrick.[4]

Mr. Floyd.
If in the Convenientest place then tis not Contrary. If definitively, then Contrary.

---

[1] There were a number of books written to defend the Laudian policy of moving the Communion table to the east end at the time of the administration of Communion. For example, Peter Heylyn, *A Coale from the Altar* (London, 1637) and *Antidotum Lincolniense* (London, 1637); Joseph Mede, *The Name Altar* (London, 1637); John Pocklington, *Altare Christianum* (London, 1637); Christopher Dow, *Innovations unjustly charged* (London, 1637). See Judith Maltby, ' "Contentiousnesse in a Feast of Charity": The Altar Controversy in the Church of England 1547–1640' (B.A. thesis, University of Illinois, 1979).

[2] For a discussion of Bishop Wren's liturgical innovations in the diocese of Norwich, see R. W. Ketton-Cremer, *Norfolk in the Civil War* (London, 1969), pp.62–88.

[3] William Laud, 'Speech delivered in Star Chamber, 1637', *Works*, (Library of Anglo-Catholic Theology, VII vols.), V, p.57.

[4] See question 3. *C.J.*, II, p.16.

Sir Iohn Strangwayes.
Edward 6 time. Care taken by Lord Bishops. 5 reazons not an altar
in Foxes booke. Knowe whether better reazons by those that have
altered it, then those did it.

Mr. peard.
Two woords added in Cathedrall & parochiall Churches.

sir william massam.
An Iniunction that the Table stand at the wall by the Bishops of
Norwich.[1]

p.121 Sir Ralph Hopton.
Two woords make it cleare removing it & officiating at it as it stands.

Mr. Dyet.
Generally or limited to time. For by the Queenes Iniunction it is to
be placed in the place of the Altar, but in the time of the Communion
to be removed.[2]

Sir Anthony Erby.
That it is by Mountagues Bishop of Norwich his orders to be fixt to
the wall.[3]

Mr. Treasurer.
Noe time to attend the Committee. Perusall of the paper. That in
Cathedrall churches the Altar stood as altar. That the Kings chappell
is involved. As it goes generally I must say Noe.

Mr. waller.
Noe difference to make obiection. May not wee be askt what latitude
this hath Being not Contrary to the Rubrick but by way of limitation,
& if wee allowe not that liberty to the governers of the church, what
shall wee.

---

[1] See above, **p.15**.

[2] '... saving when the Communion of the Sacrament is to be distributed; at which
time the same shall be so placed in good sort within the chancel, as whereby the
minister may be more conveniently heard of the communicants in his prayer and
ministration, and the communicants also more conveniently and in more number
communicate with the said minister, And after the Communion done, from time to
time the same holy table to be placed where it stood before' ('The Royal Injunctions
of Queen Elizabeth, 1559', *Visitation Articles and Injunctions*, ed. Walter Howard Frere
(London, III vols.), III, p.28).

[3] Richard Montague (1638–41) succeeded Mathew Wren (1635–38) as bishop of
Norwich. See R. W. Ketton-Cremer, *Norfolk in the Civil War* (London, 1969), pp.124–
28.

Mr. pymm.
It is onely for removing not That it might stand with the Rubrick.
Rulers according to lawe, & not to Rule us as they please & make
rules, not execute those which are made. If wee allowe that there
may be differences amongst the subiects & will take away unity &
uniformity.

Mr. waller.
Explane himselfe. Wheere the Rubrick leaves a Latitude sombody
must prescribe a place els the parish divided amongst themselves.

p.122 Mr. Cage.
The Saying 'wheere morning & evening prayer is usually sayd' does
restraine it.[1]

Sir Henry Mildmay.
A law in Athens to leave all preambles an[d] come to the matter: if
speake to all what voted, all things come not into memory at once.
To the Cannons.

Sir walter Earle.
To the orders of the house the gentleman knowes I honor him but to
the priveledge of the house, not to speake to what is voted by the
house & resolved.

Mr. pymm.
Would have the Chappells of universities put in, whence is a fountayne
of ill spiritts flowing to all parts.

Sir Hugh Chalmley.
Hee cares not which way it stands but to the matter of bowing to it
[the altar], offence.

Sir Henry Mildmay.
Moves nothing against religion but when hee knowes wee fall upon
that which wil be disputed. Tis fitt to prepare for them. Offers an act of
parlament leaving power in the king. Metropolitan & Commissioners
eclesiasticall to alter & add such further as may be for the advance-
ment of the reverence of Gods service. In for that those woords will
ground sufficient authority to warrant those Ceremonies.

---

[1]'The Table having at the Communion time a fair white linen cloth upon it, shall
stand in the body of the church, or in the chancel, where Morning Prayer and Evening
Prayer be appointed to be said' (*BCP*, 1559, p.248).

p.123 Mr. Crewe.

It doth not yet appeare that the king did ever authorize it. Whether those woords be onely restrictive to the Queenes person or to her heyres & Successors.

Mr. Ball.

The statute in Force. The woord 'King' does extend without it be limited to him during life. That it is resolved can make Cannons. That the woords 'contrary to the Rubrick', for all that bynds is but the difference syde or end. Propound it removing in severall churches & chappells. Contrary to late practize.

Mr. Controwler.

Answer to whether the statute shalbe. Noe Roabe shall resolve mee, but that what is divolved & setled by act of parlament in the King shall & disputed but with a great trenching on his majesties prerogative & right.

Mr. Boswell.

Not to be Confined to churches, & chappels in universities. Inconvenience all one. Many chappels belonging to one church. Fitt that they should have chappells, same inconvenience to chappells. That the priveledge the mother church inioynd may be in the chappells. Question, that one head of conference that the removing of Communion Tables & setting them Altar wise in many parish churches & chappells, in noe universities at the East End of the church.

p.124 Sir Beniamin Rudyerd.

Not appearing hee would present nothing appearing & not resolved by this house.

Mr. vaughan.

Noe thing more in properly proposed then to enquyre of that wee have not looked after, nor knowne not whether authority or noe. Till wee have enquyrd.

Mr. whithead.

To passe this over till authority appeare.

Mr. pymm.

If wee see an innovation, let them that iustefy it, let them produce it.

Mr. Floyd.
That if it be Contrary to late practize.

Mr. St. Iohn.
To be put to the question. For the act: desput if 'I' or 'noe'. What if wee fynd innovation, perhaps from the Bishops onely. Why not to the question.

Mr. Hambden.
These Complaynts arize not from our selves but petitions, from all parts. Many scrupled, many gone, fit to Complayne never assent to declyne it. Not to dispute it by what authority but as done & put it to the question.

Mr. Hollis.
Not large enough, removing that enioyning might be added.

Mr. Speaker.
That revooving doth not exclude enioyning.

Mr. peard.
Last clause out, & put in Contrary to the practize since the reformation.

p.125 Mr. pymm.
Let them goe without those woords because wee would not put our selves to prove of many particulars.

Resolved soe upon the Question.

Mr. pymm.
If Images more exception against them in Cathedrall churches then others they may sooner infect churches then *e contrario*. Images have bin called the Lay mens bookes. Those churches are for Cannons & Scollers, & lesse need such bookes.

3d Question. That setting up Images, Crosses & Crucifixes in Cathedrall & parish churches & chappells, shalbe another head. Say 'I'. Commissioners, Noe.
4. Question. Refuzing to administer the Sacrament to such as will not come up to the Rayle. Resolved 'I'. Commissioners answer, Noe.
5. Question. As many as are of opinion that one of the heads be The making & inioyning of the Articles at vizitations without any authority then the Bishops of the Diocesse. Resolved 'I'. Commissioners, Noe.
6. Question. One head of Conference. Whether suspending molesting,

depriving godly & Conformable ministers for not yeilding to matters inioyned without warrant: instanced in such as have bin deprived & suspended for not reading the booke of recreations.

Sir Nevill Poole.
Enough of this already, moves to wave the rest.

p.126 Mr. pymm.
Not to Complayne criminally whyles indefinite but this as a Crime must be both in Ecclesiasticall & Civill, & if a Crime this house not shewe feare to lay a Crime on any man that is found Criminall. Soe reserve to the house power to proceeed as call shall requyre.

Sir Iohn Culpeper.
Wee ought to take notice of a Crime. Observe that Common Fame bin cause & our petitions have not full proofe.

Sir Iohn Hotham.
Not feare to call that a Crime for which theere is noe lawe nor Command. Those that have broke our lawes, which are our life, let us never feare to pronounce them Criminall.

Mr. vaughan.
Does not beleeve wee should call it a Crime to suspend ministers. Why not aswell any iudgment in Lawe called a Crime as this not regarded.

Mr. Holbourne.
For matter of greivance agree, Crime spared. A Crime not what not fitt, for he conceives it noe lesse then a *premunire* [*praemunire*] & to determine that without lawe dangerous.

Sir Robert Harlowe.
When wee goe soe Hygh as to call a Crime a crime, let us lay a *premunire* upon it.

Lord Digby.
I beleeve it a Crime, but whether sufficiently debated for the honor & gravity of this house to declare the Crime.

Sir walter Earle.
Move it goe on the tearmes as before & noe question.

p.127 Bookes, & tenents.

Mr. pymm.
That it may be propounded at the Conference to make use of what
wee have, & after as the reformations come in to the Committee.

Mr. Lenthall.
That disputes must be in the universities.

Mr. pymm.
That the Doctor of the chayre hath held the Contrary.[1] & the dis-
putants may hould the tenets of the church, & then overuled accord
to the tenent of theyr church.

Dr. Eden.
Determining rather then disputing. Which he would have determing
popish tenents contrary to our church. Instance that Innocens may
marry after separation. That they may not is a popish tenent. Both
may be resoled by the university. Soe.

Question resolved 'I' noe man opposing.

Dr. Farmere.
One particular instance, is for the Citty of Lincolne, serve for that
Citty, if the greivance great they would not have sent men. 14 or
15 churches. Poore noe minister. Iurisdiction, some to Bishop [of]
Lincolne, some to the Deane & chapter. If it may be noted whoe &
wheere.

Sir Iohn wray.
Will represent in time the greivances in the County in that particular.

Sir Anthony Irby.
That enough Confessed 14 churches, but one sermon.

Sir Thomas Barington.
If it be enioyned, will drive many good ministers from, executing
theyr functions.

---

[1]Possibly John Cosin, master of Peterhouse and vice-chancellor of Cambridge university (1639–40). The vice-chancellor of Cambridge usually took the chair and
moderated the divinity acts. W. T. Costello, *The Scholastic Curriculum at Early Seventeenth-
Century Cambridge* (Cambridge, Mass., 1958), pp.15–17. I am grateful to Dr John Twigg
for his help with this problem. See his 'The University of Cambridge and the English
Revolution, 1625–1688' (Cambridge Ph.D. thesis, 1983), p.237.

Lord Falkland.

Articles enquyring whoe did it not.

Question: whether preaching, printing or enioyning to bow to the Altar shall be one head of Conference.

p.128 Question: Another head restraining Conformable ministers from preaching in theyr owne chardges.

Resolved 'I'.

Sir Thomas Litleton.

Call'd up by my Conscience, in the list one omitted: a monastery erected in the metropolis of this Kingdome. Men flock. A little army of Baalls priests swarming in this towne.[1] In the universities, in oxford one planted there. Dishonor to God & misery to this Kingdome if this whoore of Babell shall begin to pranck up her selfe.

Mr. Controwler.

Noe man he hopes will sweepe away all Ceremonies, such as new or superfluous & cannot welbe borne. Give way to represent to the King: Take notice that noe divine necessity in the constitution. But being applyed in obedience may be admitted. As he in his Conscience, soe I offer as the Governors doe not bynd by iniunction. Soe that there may be a regularity & uniformity. That one diocesse may not differ from another, move for a uniformity in things prescribed. Later part: not to restrayne the Queene in her religion, but that subiects in noe relation to her service doe abuze the liberty. The King wilbe as ready as wee to restraine it.

Mr. pymm.

That the good motion should not dye. Masse said in the university, complayned to the chauncelor & answeare was that it had such Countenance from above they could not proceed.

p.129 Questions: That theere shalbe a reservation to add more particulars as occasion. Resolved 'I'.

Shipmoney: *In foro conscientiae* satisfied but how to proceed to the Legality hee knowes not how to be satisfied.

Mr. Speaker.

Not that wee shall vote it but argue if first then vote.

[1] II Kings 23:5.

Sir Iohn Hotham.
Tis of weight, Roabe speake to it & prepare. Let it be tomorrowe.

Mr. waller.
Whether as a greivance, or as illegall may be not this moveth.

Mr. pymm.
If not illegall why doe wee then Complayne of it.

Mr. vaughan.
Out of the way if to our orders, fynd it declyned as a greivance, &
to goe to the Legality tis poynt blanck to contrary to the resolution
of all wee have done. A Time appoynted to see Records & state a
Case.

Mr. Kerton.
If it be not illegall wee will never goe about to take it from the King.
Wee must theerfore first debate it.

Mr. St. Iohn.
That not to determine to morrowe whether legall or noe, but to enter
into the debate.

The clearkes to take Coppyes & order for the tomorrowe.

Sir Thomas Fanshawe.
That Coppyes are Ready.

Mr. Hambden.
Feare that the Committee is *sine die.* Move they may followe it this
afternoone & prepare the Case.

p.130 Sir Thomas Barington.
Doubts not but the long Roabe will prepare a Case.

Mr. Lenthall.
Almost impossible to be done in that time.

Sir peeter Hammon.
Wary to state the Case, theerfore let it be as it is adiudged upon the
Record.

[Thursday, 30 April]

April 30th thursday.

Mr. wharton.
A motion for stay of proceedings in the marshalls Court. A suit begun by him selfe, the other serves him when x dayes of the parlament.

Bill of exemption woorcester & Gloucester called.

Mr. Rigby.
Divers coppyhould Lands in Lancashire, & a Bill come in. Pray to be read.

Mr. Speaker.
Move for himselfe, this a privat Bill. Ought first to attend the Speaker.

Sir Iohn Culpeper.
A petition concerning shipmoney: for Committing the Collectors because they would not pay the money before they could receive it. Rolph[1] against Bromfeild[2] unlesse he would pay £50 more then he received would commit him, which hee did. Sent his partner to him. Lay six dayes not to depart unlesse £60 more then he had received.

Mr. peard.
Calls on the Bill that Ministers should not be Iustices of Peace.

Mr. Hyde.
That a Committee of Trade be apoynted.

Sir Iohn Stangwayes.
That all the Burgeesses of maritim & port Townes be of it.

p.131 Mr. George.
Bill of Subsedies, Tonnadge & pondage, Encrease of Customes. That the Committee may surveigh the Booke.

Sir Ralph Hopton.
Trade of wooll as Considerable as any trade. Move that all that come may have voyces. Tuisdayes & Thursdayes.

---

[1] Cf. 'Walter Oke' in *C.J.* and Cope.
[2] Sir Edward Bromfield was Lord Mayor of London at the time of the complaints described in Oke's petition (1637).

Petition. Of the Merchants vintners. By Alderman. Abell Spanish Merchants inioyned to Sell. Abundance at the Kings pryce. Pray liberty to dresse meate & sell at a penny a quart.

Sir Roger North.
Bill of Aparell. Easily parswaded to lay away our bravery in these dayes. Give it a day. Severall Committees appoynted at a time destroyes all business.

The Bill of Aparell.

Mr. pryce.
To add to it Bone lace.

Mr. waynsford.
To reduce us to a fashion.

Mr. Kerton.
To add to the Committee to consider of bringing in Spanish wooll; & noe cloath to be made but of English wooll.

Mr. waynsford.
Spanish wooll like bringing in Barbara horses. I knowe not how trade stands, move the merchants may have time to bring in theyr.

Vassall.
Noe Hinderance, fyne wooll vents our wooll. Prohibite it heere, they will carry it into Holland, & take away our trade.

Mr. whithead.
Hinders our Lams wooll. If wee stay Fullers earth, can doe noe hurt to us.

p.132 Sir Nicholas Crispe.
Spanish wooll is made into manefactures which gayne exceedingly & advance the trade. If it goe to the low Countries they have vented & made there 30000 Cloaths the last yeare.

Mr. maynard.[1]
Upon the order to prepare the Busines of shipmoney. Mett, Reports seene. Mr. Hambdens Records & the Kings letters to the iudges, for theyr iudgments. Reads the Case & the resolutions *verbatim*, the King's

---

[1] Maynard's report is absent from the *C.J.* and Aston's account is much fuller than the one in Cope (p. 184).

quaere. The iudges resolutions *verbatim* read. Opinion the good & safety concernd, the whole Kingdome in danger. &c. That he is the sole iudge of danger & when & how to be avoyded. Touching Mr. Hambden's case. 4to August 12°. Thus Recytes the writt paid pardones &c. The whole woords of the writt. Commands them or theyr alleadgance to provide a ship of 400 Tun. Power to assesse within 30 dayes. To the officers to assesse according to theyr power & abilityes. *A Certiorari* returned into the Chancery Hamb. 20s. By *mittimus* into the Chequer. 22° March. *A Scire facias* out of the exchequer. **p. 133** Mr. Hambden appeard. Pleaded iudgment given against him. Propound this question to the house whether the Kingdome in danger the King's maiestie &c.

Alsoe this case. Whether the King may as in the question propose to the iudges may Command a ship &c. without Consent in parlament.[1]

Mr. Speaker.
Reads the last order. Heare the Report. Reads the head concerning shipmoney. That if wee hould it not illegall why doe wee complayne.

Mr. Crewe.
Moves that the Reporter may put it. He Recytes the state of the Report.

Mr. Maynard.
Whether upon the Case of Mr. Hambden &c proceed at large. 2d. Whether the good & safety of Kingdome in danger may without Consent of parlament &c. Great silence argues matter of weight.

Mr. Speaker. Report.
That the Committee vote the Legallity first. Then move that iudgment given, Concurrent to the opinion of all Iudges, which *prima facia* carryes it, theerfore to proceed against a iudgment wee must give reazons.

Mr. Grymston.
A iudgment in exchequer maior part of Iudges, discrepancy in opinions after iudgment. Opinion desired, report that all had delivered the opinions to know of the iudges if they had altered theyr opinions.

[1]See above, **p.130**.

p.134 Mr. Iones.
That the opinion of the Iudges was precedent to the iudgment.

Mr. Grymston.
The Case put before. & to deliver at Sessions theyr opinions which drewe men to pay after the opinions enrolled, upon iudgment of Mr. Hambdens, Case did alter theyr opinions. Desires to know reazon how & why altered.

Mr. Lenthall.
Difficulty out of what moved. Iudges have subscribed. If to put them to mayntayne what they had done upon a Rock.

Mr. Rigby.
Great woorke of the day of the time. First necessary to examine, then to vote, then to the legality, ells stayes all proceedings. Consider 2 proceedings extra Iudciall subscription by all. Maior part deliver. They subscribe for Conformity. This not to lead our iudgments. 2d Iudciall act which went in the Coulour of a Legall tract. Stands on it owne legs *prima die* in proceedings in the treaty. First the Legality to examyne, to vote. Needs noe long debate. Not new. Discussed 6 yeares, arguments known. Either Legall or illegall, by Common or statute Law: if by Common law, long, if by statute not to the Long Roabe whoe may have more reading, more lawe. The members of this house iudges of reazon, if precedence acts have determined.
p.135 1. *magna charta. Nullus Liber homo.*
2. *De Tallagio non concedendo.* Expresse the poynt. If full woords, this house may iudge.
3. 14.E.3. Noe ayd chardge or other such thing shalbe leavyed of the subiect but by act of parlament.
4. Petition of right which is fresh in our memory & these may lead us to give our vote.

Mr. peard.
That cleared by Common Lawe. Statute & reazon, noe Burthen as Treazon to invade the kings prerogative as property to the subiect which to invade is a trespas. If one, without limitt. The Common lawe not for time but for perpetuity, if Kings as immortall as Kingdomes, wee might trust. But a King may arize, may invent it to ill use. Difference twixt freemen & villaines, he hathe body free, goods free. If this hould, are wee not in the state of villenage, tennants at will. Property in Genesis: Abel had property in goods. If Kings ordayned to protect our goods they cannot despose. Common lawe appoynts a Certainty: *aut Costum aut nihill.* **p.136** Common lawe cleare. Sir Iohn

Fortescue: *Rex qui est caput corporis politicii*. All Ages have taken it soe, why have all kings els not take this way, they had good Counsellors. 50.E.3. Lord Latimer questiond for laying impositions on the subiects, fynd & imprizond. R:2d time all Concluded noe ayd. H:6 that had Tonnadge & pondage. H.4th first for life. All Kings since suitors to both houses for it, 8 Kings Raignes. Statutes more 25°E.i. that the King graunts for that for noe busines heerafter any ayd shalbe graunted but by consent in parlament the saving to preserve Townes. Theerfore *Tallagio non concedendo*: is soe full that noe exception. 23.E.3d 25.E.3. much to overthrowe. Noe man compeld to lend money because against the liberty of the subiect. 1°Ric. 3d Because they were compelld to lend money, noe such chardges nor benevolence whatsoever. **p.137** That dams Benevolences & all such ayds. The woords of the statute observes that benevolences were servitude. They were exactions, the face of Iacob but they have the hands of Esua [*sic*].[1] If all these too weake, petition of right, deny to rights us. It may be considered as statute, as Common lawe. In vayne to say Common Lawe which 45°E1. That theerfore the Queen was within the statute, if shee had not bin within the statute, a Hole had bin left for the cleargy. Then as a statute is not shipmoney a chardge. As a parlament the phistition of the Commonwealth. The iudges the Apothecaryes that administer & must not mix a drug of thery owne: Consider the disease. Provok spayne, France. Commissions as large to enforce men, some imprizoned. If then those damd [*sic*] now abolished against naturall reazon. 1. To the sheriffe, he to make the assesment. May rate as he please or favour. 2. The writt to lye in prizon *usque aliter ordinandam*. **p.138** If he be committed he is not to come out if hee would pay but till *aliter ordinandum*. The time from 4th August till 18th of March. Parlament might have bin called & wee should have given cheerfully. Tis a declaration, an execution a iudgment. Causes Concerning greivances in generall if wee have noe property, noe man will marry that cannot leave his estate, noe man industrious if not sure to enjoy his labours, noe man sowe he may reape, but not sure to sowe. Noe may provid for a daughter, nor bring up a sonne at university, but must pay shipmoney. Noe man eate but in danger to have his meate taken away or to be taken away from his meate.

Mr. Fynes.
Moves That it may be voted whether wee approove the questions reported before debate.

Speaker Reads the Questions agayne.

[1] Genesis 27:22.

Sir Iohn Evelin.
Not to the body of the busines. Whether wee may not determine to remove the extraiudicall iugment out of the way. 2. Whether a iudgment in a particular case shall Bynd in a generall.

Mr. vaughan.
Move such a Course as to see an end of it. Many that cannot speake to it suddain.

Mr. pymm.
That men cannot enforce one anothers reazons, & tis most proper.

p.139 Mr. Hambden.
Not to looze time. 1st for freedome of debate. Then to resolve that those may be the questions. Noe man to be surpriz'd.

Mr. Treasurer.
Two Committees, 2 severall Reports. What ever in time not ripe for a Committee. Noe man can deny that there has not bin a iudgment & that those come to be discus'd in the Legall ordinary way. Make a motion with a good heart: having gone soe far into debate, to call the kings counseil to heare what they can say.

Mr. Harbert.
Forward as any man to put this into a way. I was of the sense of them that moved for a Committee. A resolution to goe to the Lords on these heads. Setled religion first. Wee avoyded poynt of right; upon the act of parlament concerning the Commission. Then to goe upon the Legality, This is as farr as wee have yet gone. Before wee have stated upon what wee will debate the Kings Counsell will but hinder.

Mr. Kerton.
Press'd upon his majestie occasions. The cause concernes not the King, if a iudgment let him have it. It that be not good let the iudges answeare it.

Sir walter Earle.
To walke in the same steps our predecessors did in the petition of right, which was heere resolved & then before the Lords: Iudges & all the Kings Counsell must argue it theere.

p.140 Mr. King.
2ds my motion to state the questions first.

Mr. Secretary.
That wee should give the King the same liberty that wee have our
selves, to let the Kings Counsell.

Mr. pymm.
To heare the Kings Counsell, wee are willing & I should thinke it an
honor to this house to have them argue heare before us as iudges &
it will countenance the iudgment of the house.

Mr. St. Iohn.
That the Kings Counsell be heard. But whether wee be fitt for it, as
these iudgments stand. If this 3^{ir}[*sic*] iudged by this house, whether
wee shall admitt it as a doubt which hath bin adiudged by both
houses: not to stand with the honor of the house. *Salus regni periclitatur,
ergo*: a chardge, &c directions, & power of the writt & iudgment. This
without Consent in parlament. Then if it *in Terminis* it has bin
adiudged *quod pariclitatur* is not legall by both houses. The Causes in
the Commission of the loane was the same.[1] Sayes the safety of the
Kingdome was in eminent danger to be lost, that hee could not stay
debate. Covenant to imploy the whole money. The same in every
particular. *Regnum periclitatur*, enemyes at Sea. Poynt of time, condition
the same. In all This Commission iudged not to be Legall, by both
houses iudged not Legall. **p.141** 2d Dr. Mainwarings Sentence for
preaching sinne in them that refuz'd to pay that loane.[2] After petition[3]
sent up return'd with a Saving leaving entyre the soveraigne power
wher with intrusted for the safety protection & defence of your people.
Debated not to be admitted. Reazons presented to a Committee That
his majestie is trusted *ut Supra*. But debat as a single proposition, which
was nothing; theerfore concluded that it would reflect on the petition
& be thus Construed, if though for his purse he may not, yet for the
publique hee might & conceive these woords would be destructive,
felo de se The clause thereon waved. The Conclusion cannot lay any
&c. Commission excyse 3°*Caroi* to all the Lords to lay chardge.[4] Causes
inevitable necessity—not without hazard of king people & allyes.
Danger alike. Commission sent for. Resolved against lawe, Lords
resolved in iudgment. Cancell'd by the king, sent to the Lords. Lords
hither causes the same. All these the same of ship money.

[1]Marginal note: 'The Commission of loane'.
[2]Roger Manwaring, bishop of St. David's (1636–53). He preached a series of sermons
in 1627 in which he attacked those who resisted taxation levied by royal authority.
DNB; Russell, *1621–1629*, pp.375, 396, 404.
[3]Marginal note: 'Petition of right'.
[4]Marginal note: '2d Commission of Excyse'. For further information on the Excise,
see Conrad Russell, 'Parliament and the King's Finances', *The Origins of the English
Divil War*, ed. Conrad Russell (London, 1973), pp.114–15.

1. In poynt of iurisdiction.

2. Reflection on the thing it selfe. **p.142** Wee cald *ad tractandum et resolvendum*, If those iudgments, of this house, by inferior Courts, 12 Iudges are noe other. That mother more disconsolate whoe [*sic*] The fruits, the issue knockd in the head goes to the fundamentall of this parlament. That the houses of parlament have not power to expound the lawes: tis the first wee ever spoke, writt or printed. If not, what wilbe come of all writts of error brought in parlament when Difficulty came to Iudges adiourned to parlaments. Iudgments frequent that all parlaments proceed in Cases Criminall for lesse. That it concernes us to take notice of resolutions of parlament any thing to the Contrary.

1. Shortly. Case shipmoney stated. Presidents ready which will make the Case Knowne. If the vote of the house be that it hath once bin, iudged already by this house. I will never yeild it woorthy a new debate. If the iudgments mayntayned that in Cases of eminent danger noe taxe to be layd, then all these fall of themselves & all ells. Other Courts in honor bound to mayntayne them whyles they stand in Force. First mayntayne the iudgments of the house then wee may easily proceed.

p.143 Mr. Ball.
Dispute of a question before determined that those be the questions. That those things doe not equall this Case in question because those were extraordinary & noe iudgment. Our iudgment cannot determine what the iudges have done, before wee come to the Lords in that wee preiudicate theyr iudgment. If the house determine the Legality or illegality, then the Kings Counsell. Move for a Committee to consider of the questions.

Mr. Rigby.
Ordered that wee [*sic*].

Sir Robert Harlowe.
Concerning the Kings Counsell. Much to the honor of the house to heare them. Let us never surprize the King.

Mr. Glynn.
Moved *per* Treasurer that the Kings Counsell should be heard.[1] That Mr. Secretary sayd the King expected. Recytes St. Iohn to redeem the honor of the house the time. The Iudgment warrants the Kings iustice but this Complayned as a greivance, & now questioned in parlament, a iudgment in the Hall for the King. 3 in parlament against

---

[1] See above, **p.139**

it. Admitt the iudgment in the Hall against the iudgment, parlament in the inferiour Court against a superior. Noe end of debate. If a iudgment in the Chequer, in this & an action brought in the Kings Bench **p. 144** they resolve they must not heere it. If those iudgment be good iudgments & expressly crosse the iudgments in the Hall.

Mr. Maynard.
First to determine the question, what wee dispute on, we shalbe to seeke. If query in tearmes the same then wee had bin at an end, but if it be but by Consequences it is not fully to the Case. If wee put it upon the last poynt wee put ourselves upon a preiudice.
1. Whether to Legality.
2. To what upon questions, 3d. Whether to heare the Counsell.

Mr. Holbourne.
Necessity the Legalitee voted. 2 things wee not need not vote first as things in poynt of Ceremony: *nonsequitur*, because on the first head theerfore on this.
2. Know upon what tearmes to Confer. Say it is not legall not voted. Say it is greivous & say nothing of Legality. If wee goe & not determine it, it is such an admittance as will stop our mouths heerafter. Practize uncontrouled of the last parlament same now.
3. Query if the Kings Counsell be heard. Not of necessity, in this house supposed wisdom of kindness. May be a disadvantage to the subiects. That which moves most men least wee heare the complaynts of our Countrey onely, & the Kings Counsell. **p.145** Wee are that Body that made the acts, & for any man to tell mee my meaning, wee are one body though different in time. Not against the hearing of Counsell, but where; he is for it before the Lords. If wee admit it the Lords must expect the like which, must looze time. Object not to the mayne because resolved before. To heare whether those by the Cases or noe were to heare a Cause by parts, which were extreme preiudiciall. If he held those as cleare as proposed not with the honor of the house to heare them debated. Counsell heard at the Lords but not now.

Sergeant wyld.
2 heads whether Legality disputed or hould to the other iudgments to declyne Legality if possible. Wee cannot properly say petition of right an act of parlament, but is as binding to the iudges as acts. That wee may explane our owne acts. A iudgment that the Law should be expounded by the Law Makers. House not to be tyed to the time of the kings counsell.

Mr. Iones.
I know in reality it was adiudged before. But when wee take into Consideration all the statutes cited, & [sic].

p.146 Mr. Crewe.
Mentioned 2 iudgments wee must take that into Consideration. First, though not expresse in the poynt.

Mr. St. Iones.[1]
Not that the woord 'ship money' was in the presidents, but that the same reazons the same motive were adiudged in those cases as in this.

Mr. Harbert.
That they may have further time.

Mr. pymm.
That hee may speake with the Kings Counsell to see if they be ready.

Mr. maynard.
That such a thing may not stick upon us that an order was made to heare the kings Counsell at large & noe time limited.

Sir Thomas witherington [sic].

Mr. Lenthall.
Whether wee make not a party betwixt the King & the Kingdome. The King must defend the Kingdome, wee admitt if wee call in the kings Counsell.

Sir Hugh Chalmley.
Neither satisfied for time nor place fitt for to heare them. The gathering runs on.

Sir peeter Hammon.
Submitts to the Counsel, time Munday. Enter it soe as expected from the king.

Mr. waynsford.
As Gratious to us, soe wee meete that Grace by admitting his Counsell.

[1]Presumably Mr. St. John.

p.147 Mr. Hambden.
Understood that wee should debate the Legality. It hath bin excepted against, is not yet resolved & to heare the kings Counsell, but first to declare by vote of the house that wee are resolved to debate the Legality of it.

Sir Iohn Hotham.
Every man will give his Countrey good satisfaction, in proceeding to the quicket way. Therefore would have the Legality voted first by the house & then to heare the Kings Counsell.

Mr. pymm.
Not bynding selfe on any resolution to what wee will doe when it is heard. I shall rather desire to heare the kings Counsell first & then to expressing opinion.

Mr. vaughan.
Not yet ready for it, because not resolved upon what to goe. Mr. Hambdens Case is a Case as he by denieing hath made it. Not as wee shall goe upon the generality. There wilbe more matter for the releefe of the subiuect then strictly to his Case.

Resolved to debate the Legality. Resolved the King's Counsel to be heard if the will by Munday.

Mr. Hollis.
That wee should begin with the debate of the presidents cyted by law, St. Iohns.

Mr. pymm.
If the Counsell cleare it not.

p.148 Sir Francis Seymar.
Whether wee should limitt the Counsell wheere to begin or noe, but whether the house shall not begin to morrowe wheere they left to day.

Ordered soe.

Mr. Hambden.
Desires to be excus'd from fetching the Records from the iudges, as not proper for him.

Mr. pymm.
That he desires Hambden excus'd & the Long Raobe[s?] to fetch them.

[Friday, 1 May]

p.149 May Day.

Sir Thomas Barington.
That the day of receiving the Communion may be put of till after the fast. The Lords having not yet resolved.

Mr. Rowse.
That all that are not sworne to the oath of Alleagance & supremacy may be sworne. & theyr names & Countyes given in by the clearke.

An act read against Needle makers. Read 2[d]time.

Mr. pymm.
Moves that Mrs. Bastwicks petition may be read. Moves to have Counsell assigned her.[1]

A petition of Sir peeter vanlor against Dr. Litleton.[2]

Mr. Pelham.
That a Bill for Recoveryes by infants trusted to him may be considered on Munday.

Mr. peard.
That Sir I. packington waved Alesbury.[3] A newe writt went out, 2 returned. Move that one may forbeare to sitt till the Case decyded.

Mr. Hambden.
That a subcommittee be ordered to Consider of such Iudentures as are double Returned, that the members may be admitted.

---

[1]Susanna Bastwick. Her husband, Dr John Bastwick, was released from prison by the Long Parliament. *D.NB.* See *C.J.*, II, p.17.
[2]For the text of the petition, see Cope, p.287.
[3]Sir John Pakington was returned for both Aylesbury and Worcestershire. He chose to sit for the county in the Short Parliament. In the autumn elections, faced with opposition from 'parliamentarians', he was content to sit for Aylesbury. Keeler, pp.35, 72, 292–93; *D.NB.*

Mr. King.
To a Bill. About Fees in Hygh Commission & Ecclesiasticall courts.[1]
To pay for processe. A certainty appoynted. That the apparators to
be set in the pillary.

p.150 Dr. Eden.
Noe body excommunicated unlesse &c. as before. Noe excum-
munication but in one case. That there is *Excummunicatio legis* wheere
the statute lawe allowes excommunication & there it is in many cases
excommunicatio hominis, which is never but *propter contumaciam*. Cyte him
he is *in contunacia*, appoynt him to pay money, he is excommunicate.
A Legacy of £500 not payd, excommunicated. A Tyth pig excommunicate. Contempt the greater by how lesse the offence.

Mr. Iones.
Remembered Sir Edward Cooke, His opinion in his time not to be
granted on all occasions. Observes the diff:[*erence*] betwixt the mercy
of the Common & Civell. By the Common Law, take him Iaylor. By
the Ecclesiasticall, take him divell. The Contempt is all one but wee
maynot apply it to particular petty occasions.

Sir Thomas With.[2]
That *Contumacia* includes all things that can come in that Court. It is
fulmen Eclesiae ut lagis in some cases is admitted at Common Lawe:
but tis not equall punishment. And *excommunicetur qui conversatur cum
excommunicatster*.

Mr. peard.
If money be due to mee, as a pig to a parson, Summons *captio exigencia
proclamations secur*. Counte dayes: There is time & it must be a great
neglect. But the Civill Lawe summons him by one that cannot read
& if he appeares not, dams him. Noe man for adultry &c excom-
[*municated*] without 3ir admonished should be excommunicate according to the ould Rule: 1. *admoneas* 2. *dic eclesiae* 3. *Traditor Satan*. As
they had theyr authority from Caesar let them acknowledge theyr
Authority from Caesar.[3] Let them hould it under the great seale.

---

[1]Probably the same as 'An Act for Reformation of divers Abuses in Ecclesiastical
Courts...' The bill was committed. Aston's account gives details of the discussion of
the bill. See above, **pp.115–16**.
[2]Probably Sir Thomas Widdrington.
[3]Matthew 22:21; Mark 12:17.

p.151 Sir Ralph Hopton.
The Bill too short because it is confessed that excommunication is
allowed by the Common Lawe. & the ordinary ought in such cases
to sue out the *excommunicato Capiendo*.

The act of Administrations read agayne.

Mr. Rumzey.
Noe provision in it for disposing the estate amongst the younger
children. Administrations first granted to pray for theyr soules. Now
noe purgatory, soe noe need of that prayer.

Mr. Maynard.
The administration hinders not distribution, provided by Bills apart.
Reazon why stand to be the heyre, fitter to him that is responsall then
he that is not.

Mr. Controwler.
That if the Eldest sonne come in due time.

Sir Thomas Wither.[1]
A good Bill. In it Care & enumeration of all parties. There may be a
Case wheere none in the Bill (as a man may dye without chyld, heyre
or an heyre not knowne). As the lawe gives land by escheate to the
Lord, soe the goods to the Lord to be paid to the churchwardens for
the poore of the parish.

Mr. Bridgman.
Intention that it shall passe to the issue, kin[d]red & Legatees. A man
dyes in debt that are *bona paritura*, which in such a legall way 1/2 yeare
may expyre that time may be limited. Inconvenient to the eldest hee
a waster & may release debts.

p.152 Mr. Nerbon.
Provides well for heyres. But in case of incertainty, too much power
in the ordinary. Not usuall to dye without heyres. A Bastard has noe
heyres. In such cases that it may be as by Mr. Bridgman.

Mr. Iones.
Doubt if a Bastard dye without heyres. Query: to whom the goods to
goe. A great Question if not to the King. Which hee will not have
concluded by the Bill.

[1]Probably Sir Thomas Widdrington.

Sir Robert Crane.
That the goods of such as are poore may not be spent by the ordinary.

A Committee to consider theo [*sic*]. All common & Civill Lawyers of the house.

Mr. pymm produces a piece of a Sermon preached at St. Maryes in Cambridge by Dr. Beale vice chauncelor in his Convocation Sermon *anno* 1635.[1] That the King might constitute lawes when what where & against whom he will. That it is his meere Grace to admitt at all any consultation of parlaments. That the Tertullian language of antiquity discused preists Altars &c must be banished & new tearmes, pastors & ministers come in place.[2] Our pastors & Curates refuzd to read the Kings declaration for May Games & lawfull recreations.[3] Silencd ministers that cry downe Sabath breaking & civill honesty advanced. It may said of us as Austin.

[Blank Space]

Tonnadge & pondage must by tyed to ifs & ands, which are his majesties as unquestionably as his majesties inheritance; & guard he or guard he not the seas they are his, as wee and, our person & our estates are his, wee have property in nothing. **p.153** The parlament give a subsidy or 2 & takes away a royall prerogative or two of much more value. They feed him as men feed Apes. A bitter blow. Touching supremacy, ioyne the people, a loade upon the parlament without whom he may doe nothing which is to bynd him under lawes whoe is above all lawes. The upper and lower howses, cannot both make a hayre, not an excrement of a King. [Pym's report of Beale's sermon ends here. He continues speaking:] That he will make good the preacher, desires it may be added to the Conference with the Lords, & referd to the Committee. Messenger sent for him presently, least hee run away.

Mr. Coomes.
To have him sent for.

---

[1] William Beale, D.D., master of St. John's College, Cambridge. *DNB*.

[2] Beale's point was that the terms 'priest', 'altars', etc. were used by early Christians and are therefore more 'primitive' than 'ministers' and 'pastors'.

[3] I.e. the *Book of Sports*.

Sir Thomas Barington.
2^dthe motion to send for him. & his study seized on, vouches president in the case of Sir Gyles mountparson twas done.[1]

Mr. Controwler.
That he may be sent for. & beleeves mr. pymm wittness sufficient, but he will stand single in these opinions. The Kings Servant in ordinary if he gett out of the way. All that are of his opinion wishes wee were soe rid of him.

Dr. Eden.
A member of the Convocation house. Cons:[ider] how to send for him.

Mr. pymm.
Wee leave a note at his lodging if he will come soe. If not proceed without him.

Rumzey.
That the vice chancelor should seale up his study, & bring his sermon with him.

p.154 Mr. Glyn.
Not ripe for sending for him. Upon a bare information, wish the moderation of this house may be taken in example, that wee send not for men upon bare information. Wheere others are in the messengers hands divers dayes & must pay fees ere they be discharged.

Mr. Hollis.
To take notice of not being forward neither to seale his study nor send for his papers, Too usuall a practize now adayes.

Mr. Hambden.
That he may have notice, from this house being a member of the Convocation house.

Mr. pymm.
To have day till Thursday next.

Mr. peard.
That monition be generall, in the meane time wittnesses prepared.

---

[1]Sir Giles Mompesson. *DNB*; Clayton Roberts, *The Growth of Responsible Government in Stuart England* (Cambridge, 1966), pp. 23–25, 29–30; Colin G. C. Tite, *Impeachment and Parliamentary Judicature in Early Stuart England* (London, 1974), pp.88–90, 92–110.

Sir Iohn Strangwayes.
Englarge it to intimate Concerning such a sermon, such a day & such
a place.

Sir Robert Cooke.
Whyles wee affect moderation let us not spin our selves to soe fyne a
thred that wee looze our busines. Moves that wee may give him notice
& send to him.

Mr. George.
Never observe in any parlament without some proofe which then
made, the Committee report it & send for him.

Mr. Glyn.
To send for him is to give him monition to goe away.

Mr. whithead.
To send if he goe then it is for this. If he goe now wee cannot say for
what.

p.155 Mr. Solicitor.
Doubt about the 'I' or 'noe'. Noe man to be in that was not in before.
You put it on a right way. The 'I' was not satisfied which way it was.
The same question must be put agayne & nothing altered.

Sir Francis Seymor.
To refer it to the speaker. *Denyed*.

Sir Robert Harlowe. [*sic*].

Mr. Rigby.
&. 3 about him were 'I' but yield to the 'Noes'.

Sir Henry Mildmay.
Wee should doe too much honor to this unhappy man to divid the
house about him.

Sir Robert Harlowe.
To the orders of the house. Not Liberty to speake any thing more
then to say whether hee thinkes had more. Hee was an 'I' but gave
it. Soe many more.

Mr. Treasurer.
'Noes' gave the greater noyze but yields it not, theerfore must divid it.

Iudges came in from the Lords. The message. The Lords desire a present Conference if the busines of the house will permitt, about somthing fell in the last.[1]

Sir walter Earle.
Was one of the 'Noes' yet would relinquish it.

Mr. Harbert.
Though the particular of noe moment yet wee must divid. For mayntayning the priveledge of the house, least wee feele it in other occasions.

p.156 Sir Ralph Hopton.
A 'Noe' to wave the question.

Mr. Hambden.
Looze time, in seeking to save it. Let us first dispatch the iudges, & send woord that the house being in urgent affayre at present as soone as they can be ready they will send them woord by messengers of our owne.

Sir Iohn Wray.
Noe woonder that he that made a division in the Church should make a division in the house.

Sir walter Earle.
'Ies' all wayes, goe out.

Mr. pymm.
Upon Bills they are to goe out for must goe to bring in the Bill that are for it.

Mr. Stroud.
That mr. Speaker had misput the question by putting the negative intention, in the affirmative question.

257 'Noes'.
148
———
109

[1]The judges were Lord Chief Justice Bramston and Justice Jones (*C.J.*, II, p.18).

The 'Ies' ordered to goe out. An order upon it. The Lords set.

[Conference]

Lord Keeper.[1]
Gentlemen. &c. Knights, citizens & burgesses of the house of Commons. The Lords command mee to let you know that they take notice of the great desire & care on your parts at the last Conference shewed for preservation of the union betwixt the houses which they entertayne with respect & are resolved shalbe requited by the like Care on theyr parts as the best meanes wheerby our Consultations & resolutions may produce a happy issue & the better satisfie his majesties expectations. Said of a dutifull account or our zeale further the united proceedings which may tend to the hapines of the Kingdome & Content of both houses. **p.157** Theyr Lordships know there are priveldges of both the houses of parlament & they are not ignorant of those distinct to eich house, that what belongs to us they never intended nor have [had] noe thought to impeach or diminish in the least degree what soever.[2] On the otherside what belongs to them they hope wee will not attempt in that they wilbe as tender to preserve theyre owne as well not to violate or breake of any of ours. It hath ever bin the Course of theyr house, & by theyr Lordships proceedings it may appeare that theyr Lordships as in duty & affection to the good of both houses, Considering the motives of calling us as alsoe the ills, calamities, & great danger hanging over our heads, if a speedy supply be not, that his majestie be enabled to prevent the dangers. The reazons inform how insupportable the chardge is like to be, how impossible to recover the losse of time, in a matter soe important. The Kings command delivered 2nd [?] in which his majestie had exprest his Care & princly desire to due all that from soe favourable, iust & gratious King might be expected & had ioyned his faythfull & Kingly promises, That our iust greivances should be heard. **p.158** That noe losse of time what could not now be performed wee should have time towards winter to finish. Theyr Lordships wittnes that his majestie gave his royall woord & are Confident of his performance. That not long after his majestie honoured this house with

---

[1]This conference was called by the Lords in order to respond to Pym's complaint at the previous conference on 28 April, that the upper house had violated the Commons' privileges by urging supply before redress of grievances. See above, **pp.109–112**. Aston's account of the Lord Keeper's speech does not vary significantly in substance from other accounts, but it is not *verbatim*. It seems likely that we have here Aston's own version made from notes taken in the Painted Chamber. It is certainly a report made by a member of the lower house, as the 'House of Comons' in the Braye Manuscripts (Cope, pp. 265–72) becomes 'our house' and 'us' in Aston's record.
[2]See above, **p.109**.

his presence to renew theyr memories shewed his reazons, that moved him to presse a speedy Supply. That His majestie then tooke notice to theyr Lordships that you had voted to treat upon three heads which were Innovation in religion, propriety of goods, liberty of parlament.[1] Theerby his majestie supposed the matter of Supply set aside which soe often & with such weight of reazons he had desired should have precedence. After gratious assurance of his great zeale in religion, & upon his majesties renovation of the memory of his promises to us for redresse of all greivances hee instance in particular in that of Ship-money which he found soe much stood upon. He did presse theyr Lordships as nearest him in honor & as much concernd as other more in interest equall in hazard perswade us how considerable it was to give his majestie a speedy answer concerning that of supply.[2] **p.159**Theyr Lordships considering the necessityes had declared that in theyr opinion on the matter of supply should have presedence & be resolved of before the other heads & theeron desird & thought fitt a Conference to incline us therto. This is all at the Conference that fell from them & this as it was iust & honorable for them, soe neither they extended theyr owne priveledges nor limitted our priveledge. Yet at Conference it seemes wee tooke exception conceiving it proceeded rather from mistake then from any thing that fell from them, which was urged in our names a breach of our priveledge. Which they knowe noe reazon for because theyr Lordships admitt matter of Supply to begin with the house of Commons as naturally & properly to begin there had not onely voted Supply but concluded to threat of that first & demand relations from theyr Lordships. Wherunto theyr Lordships express commanded [*sic*] to let us know from theyr Lordships that their Lordships not varyed from theyr owne iust reazons, nor voted any thing to the preiudice of our libertyes. **p.160** They doe acknow-ledge the Bill of Subsedy passes first in the Lower house, & is then sent up to them by our Speaker presented. Therfore as they doe disclayme any such intention soe in the Conference did disclaim not to meddle by naming time or number to but [blank space] to Confer to talke with us of supply in generall or give advice. There in they hould not at all derogatory to the priveledges or our house. As wee frequently impart our greivances. They are a Body moving in an orb nearer the royall throne then wee do, & soe liker to Communicate the secrett of estate & in fortunes & interests as like we not unac-quaynted with the Record which is by us styled the indemity of the Commons Lords & Commons [*sic*]. 9 H.4. Gloster it appears there was a Conference what was fitt to be granted. King sent for 12

---

[1]See above, **pp.63–65, 110–111**.
[2]See above, **pp.81–84**.

Commons, to know what conforme to the intentions of the Lords. Discontent at it as a derogation of theyr priveledges. To prevent which established they might commonly serve about the state of the Realme. **p.161** Provided nothing reported to the King by Lords or Commons till represented by both houses as Barrs the Lords & Commons from conferring. Soe either may severally treat of what may concerne the Kingdome. This theyr Lordships have well weighed they proceeding to have bin according to usage & Custome. Many other reazons to iustify themselves but conceive that this Record abundantly satisfy. 2^dobiection that they had broke another great priveldge. Taken notice of things in the house of Commons concerning the 3 heads[1] to be treated of to which theyr Lordships Commanded him to give this iust & honorable answeare. The King tould theyr Lordships that wee had resolved to Confer with them upon three heads naming those three, how his majestie knew it belongs not to theyr Lordships to enquyre they had it from him. If in any improper way to his eare, fault in our selves. They not meddling with what others sayd to his majestie but what hee say to them, & upon what he said to them. They conceive soe far from breaking our priveldges that on the contrary part they held it soe much theyr duty to impart to us what they understood from his majestie, **p.162** that they thought they should rather merit good opinion from us for theyr advice & care then that wee should except against them. What wee call indempuity of the Commons hath noe woord in it to condemne them of the breach of our priveldges. Theerfore must returne to theyr first grounds of theyr resolution to stir us up to iust consideration of those iust grounds on which they went. How dangerous delay is both to the Kings affaires & to the Common wealth & to take into our first thoughts the matter of supply, in respect of his majesties urgency & pressing occasions. And they held this the best meanes to preserve a good union & understanding betwixt the King & his people & the onely way to avert the publique Calamity which hang over this Kingdome & to make this a happy parlament.

[Saturday, 2 May]

p. 163 May 2^d.

Mr. purfrey, prefers a bill.[2] For avoyding suitts at Lawe. Noe Bill to be preferd in any Court till the playntiffe take oath that the allegations are true, & noe iniunctions without security.

---

[1]See above, **pp.63–65, 111**.
[2]Aston gives more information about the next four bills than *C.J.* does.

An act concerning Nonresidences, many livings or Benefices, taking Farms. Odious & pernicious in all Common wealths. Severall statutes 21 & 25 H.8 to be repealed. None to be absent above 80 dayes, living voyd except in Case of Sicknes. The patron to present, if he be absent longer. That in respect they marry. Gives them leave to take Farmes. Notwithstanding statute 21 H.8 and any Cannons to the Contrary. Avoyds onely the Future not time past. 2^d The Act for Commutation money. That an abuse in disposing the money provides remedy. That all moneyes commuted shalbe imployed to pious uses. Query *ante*.

Mr. Norbon.
Add that the oath of the Commuter shalbe sufficient evidence against the ordinary.

Mr. Cage.
That it may be bestowed in the County. Committed.

The Bill of Administrations read agayne.[1]

p.164 Mr. King.
Bill short. Must be an estate for dower which is an estate for life. Now wee know leases for yeares are passed in Dower. Soe consideration of them.

Mr. Bridgman.
Noe way to Compell a distribution. The children of those that are dead to be admitted amongst such as may sue administration. The mischeife is the ordinary tyes the party to distribute as he appoynts. Soe moves that such bondes be voyd.

Rumzey.
Noe care for parents that are poore.

Mr. Norton.
The ecclesiasticall power very heavy & pressing, well pennd to take of that power. Wants way to recover. Provide that there be reserved rationable parte *bonorum* for recovery of the estate. That those that have advanced themselves other wayes by theyr owne industry should not be debarred theyr part.

---

[1]See above, **pp.115–16**.

Dr. Eden.
From the Advocate, all power taken from the ordinary to take any thing for pious uses. Confesses the use was for the Soules sake. The reazon now is, The ordinary sees a rich man dye & it is to be presumed hee would have given somwhat to pious uses. God be thanked they were never better imployed then of late.

p.165 Sir Thomas Bowyer.
A petition[1] of Sir Edward Bishop for an election in Sussex[2] of Lord Cranfield & Sir Thomas Boyer. All inhabitants: subscribe to Sir Edward Bishop. Sir Iohn Suckling got a writt. Threatned the better sort. Offred money to the meaner sort. Left it with Mr. Cranfield & £20 to be distributed to such as would give theyr voyces for him.[3]

Mr. pymm.
Moves that one that comes in soe Corruptly should not sit soe long. Theerfore to have a speciall Committee to examyne this busines.

Mr. Iones Report.

Sir philip Mainwaring.
That the house is Thin. Troubled & Report called: ought to be heard. He appeales agayne for the Thinnes, of the members.

Report read.

Mr. Treasurer.
Would not speake but upon a Command & a message from his majesties.[4] Desires leave to make use of his paper. That his majestie hath divers times & by sundry wayes acquainted us with the urgent necessity of supply, the great danger inevitably to fall the Kingdome, & our engagement of his owne honor & the honor of this nation. **p.166** That yet he hath received noe answeare at all & therfore considing that hee hath hertofore tould this house that a delay wilbe as destructive as denyall. Theerfore he requyres a speedy answeare. His majestie being well house [*sic*] that his majestie will make good whatsoever promised to this house by himselfe or by the Lord Keeper.

---

[1]For the text of Bishop's petition, see Cope, pp. 288–89. For discussion of the petition in committee, see below, **p.200**.

[2]Bramber borough.

[3]Sir Edward Bishop was himself accused of bribery in the autumn elections. See Fletcher, *Sussex*, pp. 244, 250–51; Gruenfelder, 'Short Parliament', p. 206.

[4]The report of the Lord Keeper's speech on 1 May. See above, **pp.156–62**.

Mr. pryce.
See how necessary it is, to take into consideration to give an answer, know how things stand abroad. How in the upper house, how the cleargy, how in westminster Hall. To present in one hand our greivances. In another our thankfullnes.

Mr. Kerton.
To goe in a parlamentary way. Put the house into a Committee & weigh well what to doe.

Mr. Speaker.
This the 4th message from his majestie.

Mr. pymm.
That first this priveledge much concerned in this report, first to settle this busines & make a Committee to see the Records. Then to a Committee of the house.

p.167 Ordered. That the Committee consider the priveledges mentioned in last Conference & to thinke of a Course for redresse.

Vaughan.
I never was of chayre in my life & have an indisposition on mee, I cannot serve it.

Dr. Parrey.
The first time that ever I had the honoror [sic] to be of this house. But I have read a story of one borne dumb, seeing the Kingdome in danger spoke. When theere is soe present necessity I cannot be silent, Theere is a double necessity, our greivances stand in need of releefe. The King, of Supply. Let us not looke upon things with opticks which multiply species & make our Greivances appeare much greater then they are. Let us looke upon the church & the motives in innovations. As if there such necessity of speedy redresse, soe if they be soe great as they are paynted.[1] Church never more flourished. Let us looke upon the Common wealth. Wee exceed all other Commonwealths. Lucius Crassus an excellent orator as any was of his time & t'was observed when he was to make a solemne Harang. Cicero sayes at other times he excelled all others but that day he excelled himselfe. Let it be our care to avoyd his fate. He was soe zealous & fervent in his expressions he either broke a vayne or contracted a plurisie and dyed within 7 dayes. **p.168** Twas observed by Commines the best approved of late Historians as The greatest policy in the Queen not to declare a Seccessor. *Qui sero fecit diu noluit* & *qui cito dat bis dat.* The King ought to be releeved in his warrs.

[1]See above, **pp.63, 64–69**.

Sir Francis Seymor.
If wee consider upon what impossibltyes wee are put. How can wee give before wee have wherwith. It were more to shewe our feares then our affections. If Satisfaction in one particular of the shipmoney, they would give freely.

Sir Roger North.
T'as bin the course of our ancestors to begin with greivances. Ship money & Supplyes goe hand in hand. *Non bene conveniunt nec in una sede morantur.*

Mr. Stroud.
The orders of the house bin to goe on with 3 heads: it wee forgoe the service of God, wee had as good forgoe all as not adhere to all.

p.169 Mr. Goodwin.
To goe on to the three heads.

Mr. waller.
To know whether wee come to this Committee bound or free. If some speake theyr mynds & others say wee must onely speake to the poynt, Give or not give, wee shalbe at a short issue.

Sir Robert Cooke.
Husband time, give an account, of our actions.

Mr. Hambden.
It might be whether wee are not in our owne thoughts bound up, as that wee had resolved upon these things as absolutely necessary.

Mr. Treasurer.
If wee can hansomly drawe both those things into a petition it may be soe penn'd that I may have very good hopes of it. If not I must agayne say I must feare it. I would set a part our greivances. But if I looke further of which is the wisdome of all men to looke what must necessaryly followe. Settle things for the present by some resolution of the house.

p.170 Mr. pymm.
If there were not something in my thoughts which noe man els hath spoke, I should not have spoke. Such an answer as may expresse our duty & Thankes. The great impediment hath bin our greivances, obligations upon our Consciences which noe lawe ought to impose. That of Religion if ripe for Redresse, not set a part.[1] For ship money

---

[1]There is no mention of religion in the other accounts of Pym's remarks in Cope, pp.190, 207, even though the account in Cope, p.190, is generally the fullest.

not all, but impositions which take away the property as military chardge. Therfor the lawe of noe imposition to be layd on the subiect without assent in parlament. Two things mayne. The Kings power of warr & peace: To pry into the Kings Counsells of warr or peace were imodest, unfitt. But it as undoubtedly concernes the subiect to be iealous of being engaged into a war, the Consequence wherof they know not especially being tould of a war of soe great chardge £100000 a month, of great Consequence, hazards, of much blood. Wee ought not to desire it, but if his majestie please to satisfie us of the Causes of this warr. Wee that are intrusted by our Countreyes. Ought not to engage our Countreyes, our Selves in the darke, but wee must have some light.

p.171 Mr. Controwler.
That wee may not be like the Sunamites wife whoe would not let her husband goe on the New moone or Sabbath day.[1]

Sergeant Godbolt.
Supply a debt to our Religion, a debt to our priveledges. Wee give nothing, but from one hand to the other, his majestie Riches is our Riches. Goe by way of petition to remove shipmoney, *sine strepitu* not decyded in any legall way.

Mr. Kerton.
That he would not Not answear the Learned Gentleman [men?]. But to the Busines: shipmoney not all there are others as well as Mr. Noy[2] that could fynd out. Land money. Theerfore the property of our goods in all things, ells wee cannot set apart.

Sir Robert Crane.
To goe on with propriety of goods & give without engaging our selves in a warr. Let us give us subiects & not dispute how his majestie will bestowe it. Not to complayne of liberty because a lawe for it. Nor of religion.

p.172 Sir walter Earle.
If wee should desert our priveledges because wee have a lawe for it, by the same reazon wee may aswell desert shipmoney. I shall looke for noe blessing if wee leave out that of Religion.

Mr. Bridgman.
Learnt two things, to speake short & to speake playne English. Which is that unlesse wee give till the 3 heads be determined, wee shall not

[1]Perhaps II Kings 4:22-24.
[2]William Noy, attorney general, 1631-34.

give this quarter of this yeare. Not satisfied that wee should take notice of the warr with Scotland. Not satisfyed that [*sic*].

My Lord Falkland.
Neither proiector, nor comply to give any thing till ship money taken a way. Sever that from others & see what reazon wee should have to sever. There are noe others. But this that have the like Countenance, there is noe iudgment against us. The shunshine of a parlament will disperse those mists. Religion may be seasonably treated in time. Wee engaged into parlaments.

p.173 Lord Digby.
2 requests that if a ruder expression should slip from him, he may explaine himselfe with patience. 2 Arguments for supply, Necessity, trust. Noe conclusion because the King to be trusted theerfore, wee should give first. Noe clowne soe insensible but can apprehend this noe Argument. That our goods are ours to give in subsedy, & not to withould in ship money. Great counsels must have an eye to future aswell as present ages. Take heed least our love to our present prince should lead us to institute a president to our posterity to Rue. Twere derogation from his majestie to say wee alwayes should have soe good Rings as hee. God forbid wee should in our trust to him, give way for such presidents as may be destructive to posterity. Let his majestie, releeve our greivances & restore us to our liberty, hee then may, not onely command our purses but our hearts. Money is but the nerves & sinewes of war but engaged affections the soule of it.

p.174 Sir Iohn Suckling.
This house is the forge & the Irons are in the fyre. A prentize may strike as well as a freeman, though the sparkes fly in his face. The poynt is a narrowe roome, whether consider our selves in the first, or the Kings necessity. There is not soe inevitable necessity to repayre breaches in our house as to quench a fyre. There are Breaches in our house & fyre in the next hour. Noe question which wee should releeve first. What need wee distrust more if the shipmoney be once acquitt, the King hath given too great an Earnest to goe back with the bargayne.

Mr. Fynes.
Whether shall a man, first put on Armes, march forwards, or take care how to provide for surgeons to heale our wounds. Is danger in Scotland, take heed there be not more at home. Wee are trusted with the purses of the Kingdome but soe as with our Consciences wee may give account of the reazons wee open theyr purses, wee must be

satisfied with the Ground of that warr, or wee must not engage the estates, & lives of our Countryes.[1]

Mr. Treasurer.
A soft answer breakes the bone. Such a way may be taken as may peirce us if we doe not.

p.175 Mr. Goodwyn.
Speake to the answer to his majestie. It hath bin that Somthing hath bin given in the beginning, in the middle, in the ends of parlament.

Sir Henry Mildmay.
Sayd by a wise King a wise prophet: if, you [?] will this day heare his voyce, harden not your harts.[2] H.2. King Iohn Edw. 3^d, Supply first. *Bellum indicere et pacem inire.* Due onely to the King. Remember that when wee were too nyce, wee returned home without thankes.

Mr. Hyde.
An answer that wee are not able to give if that taken away, wee are ready for supply. If wee then proceed & sitt heere, every man heere will passe his woord. Wee will Cure those other Evills.

Mr. Secretary.
The King tells us cleerly the danger. Those abroad thinke soe too. The Lords of the upper house; they conceive it fitt. The King is content if a way may be found out equivalent to preserve the Seas & give him a subsistence like our King. & he will relinquish ship money.[3]

p.176 Mr. Harbert.
Not in a way to come to an end.

Mr. Iones.
Appeales in Rome were the restorers of theyr liberty. If ever wee speake, must speake now. The resolution of the iudges in 5 dayes wee might have damned that which is of more Latitude then the iudgment. Shall wee neglect the care of Ancestors, which was such that till this time nothing could ever be able to over rule them. If wee admitt that noe regard of statutes. If subsedies & shipmoney together the unwelcomed newes that ever came to the Common wealth. If ship money taken wee may goe to Supply.

Sir Iohn Wray.
Divisions of Reuben hearts were great.[4] Divisions of great Brittaine

---

[1]Certain features in the remarks of Suckling and Fiennes resemble comments attributed to Digby in Cope, pp.207, 223.
[2]Psalm 95:8.
[3]See above, **p.83**.
[4]Judges 5:15–16.

Resemble to a great ship: tis full of leakes. Stop those leakes wee shall bring in the greatest pryze that ever was brought in by this house.

Sir Iohn Hotham.
To give an answeare all Concurrance, but that with it alone my sense concurs not: shipmoney £12000. Coate & conduct money, £40000. Thrice as much as ship money.

p.177 Sir Iohn Strangwayes.
Wishes wee had given an account long before this day. When Sir Henry Fynch & Lord Keeper speake a message like this. Answer that all our consultations have tended to prepare his majesties supply.

Mr. Treasurer.
Necessity to trouble soe often. Would have the house clearly understand that nothing ever fell from him importing the cleere taking away of ship money. That wee should consider the reall defence of the Seas. Navigation encreasing in all parts. Cost him £230000.

Mr. Glynn.
I am resolved some things must be taken away ere wee goe to any supply. Religion, what ready resolve that, what not set by. Property not insist upon it onely in ship money, but in some other things. Declared first illegall. Coate & Conduct money not yet debated. Somewhat improper. Offer that wee will.

Sir Robert Harlowe.
That wee may appoynt a subcommittee.

p.178 Mr. pymm.
2 things in execution which if not releeved if wee suffer by.

Sir Nevill Poole.
That wee have not a property in our goods & put it to the question.

Mr. Controwler.
It is a fallacy that hee that hath noe propriety in his goods cannot give.

Mr. Mountague.
A Subcommittee to Consider an answeare.

Sir Robert Crane.
To entrust Mr. Treasurer with an answeare that till propriety restored wee cannot give.

Sir Peeter Hammon.
1300 men sent out. Some 8£20. One with another, £5 a man, which is 5 times £1300. These 2 ship money & Coat & Conduct money that wee will give.

Mr. Glynn.
Wee cannot give a Categoricall answer, 'I' or 'noe'. If wee be ask't whether wee will give wee cannot say 'I'. If wee will not give, wee cannot say 'Noe'.

Mr. King.
If wee have not the iudgment reversed wee have this yeare but an induction upon our propriety, but if this continue without releefe noe man will give any thing for Land.

Sergeant Boone.
2 questions make an end. 1. Whether to give or not. [2] If not, what we shall answeare.

p.179 Mr. Solicitor.
That when a message comes from the King, & a question may be resolved for that King by the 'I', it may be put & ought to trust the Kings party.

Mr. vaughan.
Noe question that may deceive the house. Many will say 'I', many 'noe', & many that will give noe answeare. How then shall theyr sense be taken. If such a question put it is a fallacy on the house.

Mr. Treasurer.
A Sub-Committee to frame an answer.

Mr. Solicitor.
That such a question may be put wheerin all the house may give theyr 'I'.

Sir walter Earle.
That wee are not to give an answer, conceiving supply, but a present answer concerning his Majesties supply. To propose whether wee shall give a qualified answeare.

Mr. Hambden.
It were convenient to put such a question as might be answered 'I' or 'Noe'. Would have it, whether wee are now ripe for a full answeare.

[Monday, 4 May]

p.180 Munday, May 4th.

Mr. Treasurer.
Whereas on Saturday a message[1] was sent for present answeare, which
yet hath noe other answer but that this day wee will take it into f:[*inal*]
consider:[*ation*]. To facilitate dispatch pleased upon graunt of 12
subsedies presently to be passed [word unclear] sent in 3 yeares
payable. Not to determine this session, his majestie will not onely to
forbeare the present leavying of ship money, but will give way for the
utter abolishing of it in such way as to you shall seeme best. & as by
his regall woord, releeve our greivances part now, part at michaelmas
next. A present & positive answer, noe delay.

Mr. pymm.
To goe to a Committee according to order.

Sir walter Earle.
To forbeare to enter the message.

Mr. Grymston.
To know first whether the Kings Counsell attend to argue the Legality.[2]

Sir Iohn Hotham.
That they are to offer themselves. If the mace be absent wee may
speake but can order Nothing.

Mr. Goodwin.
That a Committee can take noe notice of this without an order.

Mr. waller.
That it might be ordered that the Kings Counsell were expected &
did not come.

Sir walter Earle.
That hee would have noe mention of it, in the books being the first
president in that case.

---

[1] From the king. See above, **pp.165–66**.
[2] See above, **pp.144–48**.

Mr. Lenthall to the chayre.
Reads both the messages that on Saturday that of this [*sic*]. Ordered to consider both.[1]

Sir Beniamin [Rudyerd].
Great happynes. Considering long time, what soever wee give heere lesse taken from us. What wee give it not a gyft but a purchaze, the best bargayne, purchaze Kings affections, puchaze more parlaments. Let us soe supply the King as he may see our thankfulness. Prepared to releeve our greivances & cease our laments by which wee shall cure all diseases.

p.181 Sir Gilbert Gerard.
From the County [of Middlesex] a note of military chardge. 3 subsedies shipmoney thrice more. 12000 trayndbands renewed. 1200 more & theyr armes taken away.

Mr. Treasurer answers.
Some mistake in poynt of the Armes act, to be taken out but brought to the Confynes. That county as well spare as any reazon of the adiacency of London.

Sir Nevill Poole.
That the sense of the house was not to be confyned to ship money alone but to goe on the rest.

Mr. St. Iohn.
That if military chardges as great as ship money, monopolies as much as they. To Consider of all these.

Mr. Kerton.
Wee must looke upon our purses what wee have to give. Examyne the complaynts & see our abilities.

Sir Hugh Chalmley.
Must acknowledge his majesties grace, but till resolved whether legall or not, if not why should to pruchaze it of. Theerfore consider both the first & second message.

Mr. Controwler.
Whether legall or not the thing being taken away it will fall to the ground. Tis an act of Grace & noe bargaine in it.

[1]See above, **pp.165–66, 172**; *C.J.*, II, p.19 (2 May).

Mr. Rigby.
That the king of Grace & mercy acknowledged, But woords upon the granting of 12 subsedies, not call it a bargayne, but ensuing upon the granting. If illegall our grant a great guyft, if legall it is far too little.

Sir Iohn Culpepper.
That the Legallity & not the present pressure is that which troubles us. Theerfore to the question.

Mr. Holbourne.
Of the opinion of the 2 last. Add a reazon, necessity of it query against lawe & not rest on any newe act. As many acts as may be, one more will not make it good. Right soe inha'rent as not to be layd downe by any graunt of the kings. Theerfore against Lawe.

Mr. Controwler. [sic]

Sir Edward Mountford.
If under this Title military chardges be implyed & wee still under, then wee are noe better.

Sir Francis Seymer.
1. Question which first, supply or greivances. If but 12ᵈinstead of 12 subsedies, not give it. Have not the Lords voted supply first, will not our consent be drawn in president for the future. **p.182** A remonstrance to his Majestie, otherwise wee cannot till the Countrey satisfied.

Sergeant Glanvill.
Much about Legality of ship money, propounded that which whyles it sticks noe purpose to make any acts of parlament what soever. Rather by way of iudgment then act. Iudgment declaratory that ship money ought to be taken away & did never bynd. That the Lords & Commons declare it ought to be taken away. In 7°Iac of impositions, the king would not. Writts to the ports I doubt of that. Writts to the Kingdome in my iudgment illegall, I am sonne of a iudge & pronounce it my iudgment, a wicket iudgment. Libertyes of parlament in the first place, religion not set by: but what with libertyes of noe parlaments. Let ever [sic]. If 12 subsidies for an inheritance too poore a compensation & weakens the Titles to demand it. Monopolies. Trusted in the Bill of monopolies & resolves it cannot be mooved. Noe better lawe. They should have brought an action upon the statute, noe man might without a incurring a *preauninure* countenance it.

Others goe out of the way. Military chardges, drew that petition. The Lords then sayd there must be some releefe. The letteres if to borrowe & repay it agayne not to be soe much stood upon. 12 subsidies is not a contract. Parlaments were instituted for the releefe of Kingdomes. If wee had noe greivances, wee could not give lesse then 4 or 5 sudsedies in gratuity.

Sir Iohn Wray.
This house never had such a speaker. To buy ship money & purchaze warr noe man will give; but [*sic*].

p.182 [*A*]¹ Sir Robert Harlowe.
That wee might fall downe to our David as Abigall with teares of acknowledge[*ment*].²

Mr. waller.
Wee were in a good way. I would be glad to remoove a rubb out of the way not to purchaze warr, but to pray for peace.

Sir Robert Cooke.
In a parlamentary way to second Mr. Sergeant Glanville in that of a hatefull opinion, That no act could take away that iudgment. That the opinion was mistaken of purchazing peace. It is necessary to expresse our Duty how the pulse of the Countrey beates to it. When a King under takes a war had need of hearts as well as purses. This warr tooke heart from some great cleargy men, that stiled it *Bellum Episcopale*. What preiudice that hath done I know not. Petition that wee may petition. That his majestie had not finally shut his heart against the Scotts, soe to open the doore of supplication to the English.

Sir Iohn Strangwayes.
If cleared upon the Iudgment & that of military chardges, I shall give freely, cheerfully, & never aske him what hee will doe with it.

Sir Iohn Hotham.
Will first have it acted then give & wishes the question of Scotland had not bin stirr'd.

Mr. Hoskins.
Hath given time, hath promised not to breake the Sessions: shipmoney declared against it. Military chardges examined the authority. Rest of greivance; at Leizure.

¹Aston has two pages numbered 182.
²I Samuel 25:23–24.

Mr. waynsford.
To declare by vote that the motion of Scotland goe noe further.

Sergeant Glanvill.
Use a subCommittee to prepare a preamble to the Bill of subsedies.
Noe meanes engage this house into a warr. That wee should not be
those uzzas, to touch that ark.[1] **p.183** Let us have noe dispute about
it, but declaire it illegall absolute. Tis better live under a knowne lawe
then an uncertaine.

Sir Hugh Chalmley.
Desires to be dischardged in the ports aswell as land. A vote to be
past heere of the illegality then to give freely. Let the king doe what
hee will with it.

Mr. Rigby.
That Mr. Glanville would have the illegality passe in an act. To vote
it first would induce well to the declaration.

Sir Iohn Culpeper.
Noe man more willing to lay it by, but would first heare what may
be sayd to it.

Mr. Treasurer.
A duty every man houlds his owne Conscience, & ought to declare
it. 1st the woorke of the day next to his heart. The happy resolution
of this day the happines of this Kingdome. Wee have a time for ship
money. Difficult precedence. 12°[James] was of the house. Many Bills
past, time like this dissolution followed it. 18°[James] That parlament
broke upone the strait of time, the kingdome suffred in it. If wee doe
not the issue wilbe hazardous. If wee doe fall to the act: he feares such
an issue as wee expect will not be had.

Mr. Cage.
Some speech of shipmoney with couloure upon ports. Moves it may
have the same dischardge with the lands, for military chardges voted
whether Legall or onely as is stated by way of letteres. If that of
Religion be set a side wee shall give noe satisfaction nor prosper.

Sergeant Glanvill.
The iudgment, wee conplayne of, upon an inland writt: the vote upon
the iudgment will destroy only one. The declaration wee shall make
will take a way all.

---

[1]II Samuel 6:6–7; I Chronicles 13:9–10.

p.184 Mr. Hambdon.

Wee are come to present supply & great supply. Recytes severall motions *super milite*. Other things as weighty. Religion, consider the Consequences. Sentences of the parsons scape heere, but the sentences of [*sic*]. Libertyes of parlaments looke to the offence, but as good have none as not instituted in theyr right libertyes. Property of goods of great Consequence. The ground layd that it could not be layd downe by any act is such an opinion abroad & not layd downe wee shall doe our selves more hurt then ever wee did good. Moves that this house taking notice of this opinion may declare something in parlament, to damn such an opinion.

Mr. pryce.

Ship money is the chyld of want, of necessity. Princes never want Counsell. Vote now 4 subsedies, next yeare 4 more, 3^{d}yeare agayne 4 more.

Mr. Iones.

Every mans Soule ready to give to the King & to him alone. A generation of men that have rayzed a doctrine that the Common lawe wants reazon: parlament too strong, too Hygh, too populous. Let it be given in a parlamentary way, which never any King made any great defence but by parlament & that sitting. Our guyft applyed to him. To that of a port towne, Mr. Glanville sayd some semblance for ports: for the Cinque ports wee have it that in Doomsday. But that £36000 should come in a writt to London. **p.185** In the Edward 3^d proposed to defend the land & guard the Seas. Let the Cinque ports doe it. Difference of times, a ship of those times not considerable. That the opinion of inharence in the Crowne cannot be divested by act of parlament. Some rights cannot be divested as purveyance. To pardon to devest him of that is the 1stflowre of the Crowne, to take away his mercy. But this being against lawe. He is our protector wee to live under his protection not *secundum arbitrium* but *leges angliae*. Noe maxime but if admitt it to debate remoove the very beleefe of his foundation. Some hee hath but this is none of those, The way by act: illegall. Subsidy to the king alone without relation or limitation.

Mr. Hambden.

Argues mistaken: as he conceives upon a Ground, that in case of necessity hee might lay imposition on his people. Treasurer query wee might not declare opinion against this.

Mr. Iones.
Not mistake him, but to declare it sound.

Sir William Massam.
To Read the question concerning the generall opinion.

Mr. Solicitor.
That hee cannot offer any thing agreeable to all Sense of the house. Answer to his message, then debate, now to facilitate his message, if it cannot advance, not retard it. Query: if whether give first or releefe first. Wee dispute them before wee resolve which first. But new things put further of he speakes to that. 3ᵈthing to proced them both. Remedy of opinion fell from the iudges, not ripe, not seazonable. If weigh with supply, our greivances I doubt how to bring a by opinion fall from iudges in an argument how this can come in debate I know not. **p.186** Conceives not by any that this came into resolution or opinion at all, but if doubted in poynts lesse important. If they conceived an impossibility to save the Kingdome but by such a right. Many fall upon, religion, military chardge, pr:[*ivilege*] of parlament. It has at large noe issue, wee must put it upon present supply.

Sir walter Earle.
The way to come to the poynt was to vote the illegality. Not onely in the Courts heere, but in every sessions, that 1000 acts of parlament more in this case were voyd. Moves Mr. St. Iohns to set a foote the motion last day.

Mr. St. Iohn.
Would not speake but to the question: message of offer debate: whether legall or noe. If Legall they buy that which the King hath noe power to graunt. That not satisfyed, query, whether ship money legall or not but to the maxime that wee have a property. Noe doubt but when the defence in question all acts layd aside. If noe ship money; buyld Castles, rayze men make bridges. Pretence of good of the Kingdome, if this stand still afoote, he may lay any other; but hee propounds that unlesse wee have a Rule in poynt of property: that is such a Case wheere *solus regni periculi* not yet full. There may be other woords which may pretend soe great danger as utterly to be lost. Theerfore to Consider how farr such pretences may be stated by both houses. Would have noe new act but a Declaration of the ould Lawe.

Sir miles Fletwood.
That a iudgment in these houses with the Lords with the King, may take away the Roote. Butt when wee have done, if Religion being not

releevd from such Ceremonies enforced as are destructive to our religion; wee will lay all at his majesties feete, & releeve us in those, hee shall take any thing, but nothing conditionall for.

p.187 Sergeant Godbolt.
If ship money against the good of the Common wealth noe more lawe: Lawes.

Mr. Stroud.
Let us first set an order what wee shall speake to, one sp:[*eech*] to religion, to liberty, to property, every one severally; the king wants time & wee looze it. Order for something first.

Mr. Solicitor.
First an order to keepe them in, ells wee shall not heare it.

Mr. Treasurer.
To put us upon that poynt of supply.

Sir Peeter Hammon.
The King leaves it to us to take what way wee will to abolish it. To goe to that woorke.

Mr. St. Iohn.
That shipmoney to be layd aside upon Sacrifize of 12 subsedies: to the Question whether Legall or not.

Mr. Solicitor.
Recytes Mr. St. Iohns Question, but denyes the ground that many are against the Question. That such a question will not have the valewe they looke for. Order & power of the Committee denyes it, which is an answer to the King. Ells wee run from the state of the Question.

Lord Digby.
A friend to Mr. St. Iohns query, but not the time. Consider the query whether wee were in a capacity to give, whether the message have altered the case, for if propriety be not stated wee are not fitt to give.

Sir Ralph Hopton.
Never a query of 3 parts: middle way, proposed both goe togather. Religion have precedence of dignity, but at this time not of order. Right way whether wee might not passe togather the act of supply &

grievances. By same declaration settle priveledges, military chardges, monopolies. In a better case then hee understood.

Mr. Vaughan.
The going away a blemish to them that doe it as neglecting theyr duty to the King & Countrey. **p.188** that wee may resolve somthing for the King, & they that are absent when they come in agayne may undoe it.

Mr. pymm.
Many things not heard, discouragement in what wee shall say. Things conceived impertinent which are pertinent. To the Kings message: whether 12 Subsedies. Hee that thinkes Religion not satisfied, he that thinks property, privilege or other things left out, it is not impertinent. Unlesse wee consider the generall ground, which is pretence of necessity. If this the ground, then wee are left a greater danger then ship-money is. Which ground if not taken away, wee are never the nearer. If ship money taken away upon that ground then all fall. And his majestie to be consulted with how hee will give way to the removing those grounds. Our petition of right is a declaratory Lawe, the fruitts of that, have not imprizonments bin frequent, impositions layd. Twas declared in parlament that this intention never was that Tonnadge & poundage should be taken away. And till wee thinke of other things as well, military chardge as pressure of theyr Bodyes. If wee supply, compound for exemptions.

Mr. Glynn.
In the way to make it destructive. 2 questions make answer to either: first determine an answer to the first. Then to debate the 2^d.

Mr. Secretary.
Not 2 messages. Both one.

Mr. Bridgman.
That Mr. Sergeant Glanvill may propose agayne the sense of this motion & put to the question.

Sergeant Glanvill.
If a declaration be pennd against ship money & the grounds of ship money it will reach all. Doubts not but a Committee will penn such a declaration as may reach all which in above of 400 men will not be found out. **p.189** Somthings in debate in a parlament whether it were a parlament or not, in the same act a declaratory iudgment that may Roote out the ground of it.

Mr. Kerton.
Never any thing went to a Committee that was not first voted heere. Whether the grounds be adiudged heere already.

Mr. Speaker.
Nott fitt for voting now. But when prepared in a Bill is not that voting.

Mr. St. Iohn.
Without a Question stated wee speake to severall parts & never come to an issue.

Mr. Treasurer.
The King hath soe much to say in some of these things wee cannot condemne them without hearing. Traynd Bands have gone in Question time sitting a parlament. The King other wayes & lawes for maytaining. Sir Edward Cooke. In time of Invasion the king may come to my house & throw it downe. Lawe in Henry 4^{ths} time that wee are bound to presse & bring men to the confines. Desires wee may goe by way of petition.

Sergeant Wyld.
Whether wee have power to proceed to voting of shipmoney. That iudgment not soe Binding because 4 of them [judges] against the body of the iudgment. Though subsedie ought not to come in the forefront, yet wee may consider it & it is ripe for the question. Mr. Speaker to resume the chardge, & put it to the question.

Mr. Hyde.
Ready for a question, but not such a question as I yet heare. The message hath advanced well. Noe greivance layd by. Single out ship money & insist wholly upon that. Noe. That it shalbe soe destroyed as wee please & wee are very unhappy if wee soe doe it not as may take of all ells: Question whether upon satisfaction that shipmoney can be soe destroyed: wee shall not supply. If not; feare if wee propose not now, never propose now.

Sir walter Earle.
To put it to the Question whether it be not already adiudged.

Lord Falkland.
Not our intention to destroy the woords 'ship money', but the greivance of leavying money out of parlament. All serve God, & may all meete at the Communion: Not to desert the proprietyes for any thing yet said of Altars.[1] Moves to have Mr. Hydes question.

[1]Marginal note: 'vid. other end'.

p.190 Mr. Floyd.

I move for my Lord of Falklands & Mr. Hydes question. If there be a Curse upon them that remove Landmarkes,[1] then is a greater curse on them that give illegall iudgments. Whether upon that a greivance of shipmoney abolished, & by way of declaration, if 12 sudsedies given in severall sessions wee may not have all the dependants taken of by the iudgment.

Mr. hamden.

If wee goe downe & leave a clog [?] on the Consciences of our Countrey, wee cannot be welcome. If wee accept this as of Grace & favour wee Confesse a right. I did not give way to the dispute of the Kings Counsell but in duty & for clearnes.

Mr. Fynes.

Wee are to give an answer to his majestie. It is yet unresolved, whether to give upon the tearmes of the message, whether upon the ground of property. Whether the other parts. Sever them & debate severally, Soe come to an end.

Mr. Goodwyn.

Without a question wee shall never give an answer to his majesties question: Therfore let the question be of the legality of ship money.

Mr. Hollis.

Vote the Legality, then to the Question.

Mr. Treasurer.

The Kings Counsell was appoynted for this day to have spoke: therfore not fitt to put to the question till they be heard.[2]

Mr. waller.

It were not ingeniously done of us to put to the question before they be heard. Would have a sub committee to consider.

Mr. Harbert.

Because the king will out of his Grace & favour hasten our busines, his owne message has hindred his owne busines. [King's] Counsell being put off by pretence of debate. Noe iustice to put it to the question. Would have a question whether wee are yet ripe to give answer to that of Supply.

---

[1]Deuteronomy 27:17, cited in the service of commination against sinners: 'Minister. Cursed is he that removeth away the mark of his neighbour's land. Answer. Amen' (*BCP*, 1559, p.317).

[2]See above, **pp.144–48, 180**.

p.191 Mr. Rigby.
Would know how many times a question must be demanded & by how many men must it be demanded, before wee have it.

Sergeant Glanvill.
Kings call theyr Iustice 'Grace & favour'. Wee must not be captious at woords. Hee would have the Kings Counsell heard.

Sir walter Earle.
Excepts against the woord 'captious'; he would have it voted in poynt of the Legality.

Mr. Kerton.
If not be voted we looze the Lustre of the guyft because wee know not if Legall or illegall.

Mr. Controwler.
If sorry to see us soe nice, in that which within 2 moneths wee would soe gladly have embraced & to stand upon impertinences.

Mr. pymm.
Noe Question but to make answer to the King. The Legality of ship money is not impertinent to that Question, if the Kings Counsell desire to be heard I shall yeild to it.

Sir philip manwaring.
That wee should consider the messages,[1] a part which being short, wee shall come to a Conclusion.

Mr. wainsford.
Would have a care what should be the question, hee thinkes it wilbe the last. The King has a iudgment. Doe wee thinke to conclude that by a vote heere.

Sergeant Godbolt.
Would have a subcommittee to draw an act to abolish shipping money.

Mr. vaughan.
Would have a reazon then change his opinion, but houlds wee are not ripe to vote it now. If wee are, then say wee will supply, taking those into Consideration wee shall have time to debate.

[1] See above, **pp.165–66, 180**.

Mr. Hambden.
Not ripe for debate whether legall or illegall, but whether the not voting that be an impediment, for unlesse it be illegall it is to noe purpose to give.

Mr. St. John.
If it be legall he will willingly give 12 subsedies. If not, it is too much. Theerfore the question must be decyded.

Sergeant Glanvill.
Be it legall or illegall it is not for ship money alone, it is for all our greivances, & a promise of time.

p.192 Mr. Stroud.
Wonders whence the doubt that debate of shipmoney will advantage. If the question were upon exchange of a house & land, were it impertinent to desire to see his land, to see his title before hee change.

Mr. pymm.
Agayne to vote the Legality or illegaty [*sic*].

Sir philip Manwaring.
Query whether the question conduce to the answer of his majestie or noe.

Mr. Lewkner.
If the question were proper to be put now should be ready as any man. But appeals to the house if fit to be voted ere debated.

Lord Falkland.
Is absolute of opinion it must sometime be voted. That it is with Mr. Stroud to be first voted, but that not proper without debate first.

Mr. Herbert.
If the message beare it not, it must not be the question.

Sir Hugh Chalmley.
Mistake the question, not to vote it but whether it may not be debated before answer to the King.

Mr. Slingsby.
Voting admitts a legality, which hee never conceived the sense of the house, & to vote it being countenanced by a iudgment of soe hygh a nature as iudges them in Rebellion that deny it.

These woords vehemently excepted against, but at last passed by without recantation.

Question: whether the Legality of the shipmoney must be voted & debated before an answer to the King.

Mr. Ball.
Not knowing what can be sayd for it or against it, wee can give noe vote in it. Would have this query layd aside & to have a particular Committee.

Lord Digby.
Consider the consequence if vote it presently without debate, preiudiciall to the honor of this house. If not presently voted is it not a delay to the King. Hee would have us petition the King.

p.193 Sergeant Glanvill.
The Lords may resolve it upon bringing in the Records with or without us. When wee goe in a legall way wee must goe to the Lords.

Sir Iohn Hotham.
Conceives noe need of long debate.

Mr. Goodwin.
Noe precipitation in it being debated 1st then voted.

Lord Digby.
Wee may give a proper answer noe way preiudiciall to the business.

Sir Ralph Hopton.
Let us offer an answer by way of excuse. Then wee vote ship money not lawfull, & get more time.

Mr. Hambden.
Would have such a question to which hee might give 'I' or 'noe' cleerly.

Sir Robert Harlowe.
To have it debated before wee have give a positive answeare.

Mr. Hambden.
Would have it ordered to be debated & voted to the end wee may give the better answer to his Majestie.

Mr. Grymston.
That tis impossible to give supply till property be setled. If voted the
Legality not determined; That done wee must goe up to the Lords.
What are wee the better if they vote it not.

Sir Iohn Evelin.
If I have received wrong & may be satisfied in my owne way, what
reazon have I to seeke another.

Mr. Solicitor.
Mr. Hambdens question comes nearest the way if wee will make it an
answer & a question both.

Mr. Glynn.
Would declyne the question, it either is a flatt denyall or by consequence a denyall to the Kings question. 1: because it will requyre long
debate; 2ᵈit wilbe disadvantage & preiudice if wee have not time to
debate it, wee leave it more questionable.

Mr. peps.
That Mr. Hambdens question is but delay. Mr. Glanvill is the proper
way.

Mr. Treasurer.
Playne dealing is the best way, would know playnly if the Legality
were voted whether then wee would give the 12 subsedies.

p.194 Sir William Savill.
That hee durst answeare for his county, that if shipmoney were taken
away, they would give.

Sir Iohn Hotham.
That he knew not what authority Sir William had for that, for wheere
hee lived the Countrey[1] Complayned more of those Military chardges.
& unlesse they might have releefe, that & some other greivances they
would not willingly give.

Mr. Bellases.
That hee was for the same shire sir william Savill was, & knew not
mynd they might be of about him, but where he lived he was sure

---

[1]Hotham sat for Beverley in Yorkshire. Savile and Belasyse sat for the county.

they should not be welcome home unlesse they brought home releefe
in some other things as well as shipmoney.[1]

Mr. Treasurer.
That it were better set it in a way then run the Hazard of a breach.

Sir peeter Hammon.
Moves to revive Mr. Hambdens question agayne.

Sir Roger Twisden.
That they would be content to pay subsedies if ship money & some
other things be taken away.

Sir Iohn Strangwayes.
Hee hath heard all attentively, but cannot goe from Sergeant Glanvills
motion.

Lord Digby.
That wee may give a present & playne answere, & petition to shewe
our greivances.

Mr. pymm.
Hee would not goe by petition but to frame heads to present to his
majestie.

Mr. Solicitor.
A Committee are to frame & to forme matter given them but not to
chooze matter. Moves either for an answear or supply.

Mr. Iones.
The question of Legality wav'd because they would not have a question to which they must say noe. Wee would have noe question put
with which wee must say 'noe' to the King.

Sir T:[homas] A:[ston].
In this distraction: moved that the Speaker might give account of our
actions since wee mett that they had bin onely to enable us to serve

---

[1] Belasyse, Hotham and Sir Hugh Cholmley were imprisoned and then called before
the council to account for their remarks concerning grievances. They were released a
few days later. Upon returning to Yorkshire, they were involved in a petition presented
in July 1640 of the Yorkshire gentry to the king concerning military charges. *CSPD*,
1640, pp.130, 154–55, 166, 523–24; Sir Hugh Cholmley, *Memoirs* (n.p., 1787), pp.61–
64; A. Gooder, *The Parliamentary Representatives of the County of York 1258–1832* (Yorkshire
Archaeological Society Record Series, vol. xcvi, 1938), II, pp.46–47; Rushworth, III,
p. 1214.

the King & noe delay used by us. And that wee have taken into Consideration his Majesties 2ᵈ message, & Humbly pray a fewe dayes respite, that **p.195** we may prepare an act wheerin to passe his supply togather with out greivances & wee would leave a blanck that if wee presented such to him might drawe more from his majestie then hee expected to part with, wee might fill up the blanck proportionable to the Grace & favour the Common wealth should receive by his majesties graunt. This could give noe offence & it would undoubtedly gaine us releefe in our greatest greivance which was strait of time. And could noe way preiudice the affaires of the house. But *quos Deus vult perdere hos dementat prius*. Noe motion that was not either for a peremptory 'I' or 'Noe' would please the one side, nor the other were pleas'd with any that might imply any Consent till first theyr greivances were voted. Soe Nothing was resolved but to adiourne till the next day for further Consultation which the king tooke for a delay, which hee had concluded as good as denyall.

[Tuesday, 5 May]

[5 May, Tuesday]

& The next morning sent for the speaker, kept him with him, & then sent for us to the Lords house & spoke as followeth.

The Kings speech.
My Lords there can noe occasion of my comming to this house be soe unpleasing to mee as this at this time, the feare of doing that which I am to doe to day made mee not long agoe to come into this house where I exprest my feare & the remedyes that I thought necessary the exchuing of it.[1] I must needs confesse & acknowledge that you my Lords of the higher house did give mee soe willing an eare & such an affectionate that you did shew your selves accordingly theerafter, soe that certainly I may say if there had bin any meanes to have given an happy end to this parlament it was not your Lordships fault that it was not soe. Therfore my Lords in the first place I must thanke you for your good endeavours. My Lords for my owne part you can witnes what on the first day of the parlament my Lord Keeper sayd to you **p.196** in my name,[2] what he said agayne at the Banqueting house at white Hall,[3] what I sayd the last day my selfe,[4] I name it to

---

[1]The king made this speech to the Lords on 24 April and it was reported the next day to the Commons in conference by the Lord Keeper. See above, **pp.81–84**.
[2]Reported to the Commons on 17 April (see above).
[3]See above, **pp.34–37**.
[4]See above, **pp.81–84, 165–66, 180**.

you not in any doubt that you doe not remember but to shewe you that I never sayd any thing that way in favour to my people but by the Grace of God, I will punctually & really performe it. My Lords I know that they have insisted very much on greivances. I will not say they be altogather free though it may be not soe many as the publique voyce would make them, yet I desire you for to know agayne & now especially at this time, that out of parlament I shalbe as ready, (if not more willing) to heare any iust greivances as in parlament. There is one thing that I have heard was much spoken of though not soe much insisted on as others & that is Religion. I have expressed my selfe the last day I doe not doubt but you remember it, certainly I shalbe more careful (as I am most concern'd) in the preservation of that purity of religion which I thanke God is established in the church of England.[1] And I shalbe as carefull out of parlament as in parlament to doe that. My Lords I shallnot trouble you long with woords, it is not my fashion. What I offred the last day to the house of Commons,[2] I thinke it is very well knowne to you all, how they accepted it.[3] I thinke it aswell knowne. My Lords you knowe at the first I expressed my selfe by my Lord Keeper, that delay was woorse danger then refusing.[4] I would not put this fault on all the whole house, I will not iudge soe uncharitably. But it hath bin in some fewe cunning & ill affectioned men, that have bin the cause of this misunderstanding. I shall onely end as I began, giving your Lordships thankes for the care you had of myne honour. Desiring you to goe on & assist mee for the mayntayning of Government, & the libertyes of the people, that they soe much start at. For my Lords, noe king in the world shalbe more carefull to mayntayne the propriety of theyr goods, the liberty of theyr persons **p.197** & true Religion then I shalbe. And now my Lord Keeper doe as I have Commanded you.

The Lord Keeper then added:
My Lords & you gentlemen of the house of Commons the kings Majestie doth dissolve this parlament.

Tuisday the 6th [*sic*] of May.[5]

---

[1]See above, **p.82**.
[2]See above, **p.180**.
[3]'His Majesty finding the Parliament thus averse to the matters of Supply, which rather gave incouragement to the *Scotch* Covenanters, than put his Majesty in hopes to be able by Parliamentary assistance to bring them to Obedience...' (Nalson, I, p.342). See the debate of 4 May (above, **pp.180–95**).
[4]See above, **p.7–9**.
[5]Tuesday was 5 May.

[Committee Reports, 16 April: privileges]

These following were some passages at Committees left out of the Iournall.

p.189 The 16th of April, Committee of priveledges.

At this Committee rizes a great Controversie whether a Mayor for a towne may be of the house or not.[1] President was vouched that Mr. Lynn mayor of exeter did serve.[2] A great Caution to be had of this, least the house be filled with mayors, whoe may returne themselves. Difference proposed betwixt a mayor returning himself & a mayor duely chozen. Great dispute as that a mayore was bound to attend the towne hee had in chardge & not to leave it. Others & *Contra*, that all writts are directed to the sheriffes soe the Mayor bound by noe necessity of attendance & may serve. But this was generally opposed. Sir Henry Harbert[3] was returned for Bewdeley by the mayor & maior part: Sir Ralph Clare[4] returned by some others, pretence not poling though it was requyred: referd to tryall.[5]

Sir Iohn Davis.
Recommends a Burgesse to the Burough of Bedwin.[6] As being cheife Lord of the towne, the Earle of Hartford being stuard of the Leete recommends Sir Francis Seymors **p.199** sonne.[7] Allegation that one Francklyn an atturney detayned the warant till a new perteane [*sic*]. The day of the election choze a newe Reave & the next day after the returne of the warrant made a returne. Day was given till the Thursday after when it was alleadged that Franklyn the Stuard had gott the precept & threatened the cominalty that they should looze theyr marketts & Commons. Appoynts a leete for his purpoze. Swears the Commoners, wheeras none have voyces but onely the port Reave or those that have bin port Reves & not above 7. For none can be burgesses but such as have bin Port Reves.[8] Hee choze the Iury & manadged the election himselfe. To which allegations Francklyn

[1]See above, **p.4**. Marginal note: 'mayors not to be returned'.
[2]John Lynne was mayor of Exeter and sat for the city in 1628. Wallace MacCaffrey, *Exeter, 1540–1640* (Cambridge, Mass., 1958), p.257.
[3]Sir Henry Herbert (Bewdley). Keeler, p.211; *DNB*.
[4]Sir Ralph Clare sat for Bewdley in the parliaments of the 1620s. *DNB*.
[5]Cf. Keeler, p.73; W. R. Williams, *Parliamentary History of the County of Worcestershire* (Hereford, 1897), pp.164–66.
[6]For Sir John Danvers' remarks concerning the Bedwin elections in the house, see above, **p.104**. The disputed elections in Bedwin were reported to the Commons on 28 April.
[7]Charles Seymor.
[8]See Keeler, p.70.

confesses the receipt of the warrant, & being the Leete was not then to be kept. Desires the sheriffe to mend the warrant being not rightly directed. That the port Reave or Bayliffe being ignorant desired his assistance soe all hee did was by his Consent. That Mr. Harding had 52 voyces, Seymer 31 & cordwell 21.

Mr. Ball.
Sayd all ought to have voyce, gives his vote for the maior part.[1]

Mr. Glyn.
That there was *de facto* an officer which was good. The mandate was good. The question whoe were electors. The Lords uncertaine might transfer theyr estates, & where it is doubtfull alwayes to approve the most popular.

p.200. Mr. Maynard.
If Liberty of Elections shalbe taken away by reducing them to fewe hands, wee shall in time looze the freedome of the members.

Mr. hambden.
That In consideration there were 31 for: 21 [against]; & noe certainty appearing whoe ought to be the choozers, being never any competition had bin before. To goe with the maior part which was soe determined.

Mr. Bishop[2] was returned with 2 others: one had 11, the other 12. Hee had all 23. Not to sit till the Indenturers perused & then being found the same parties had signed the Indentures to all three, he was admitted upon report made.

Sir Humphrey Tracy[3]: A petition was preferd by Nathaniel Stephens of Gloster against Sir Humphrey Tracy sheriff of the shire for the returne of Sir Robert Tracy. Alleadging that Stephens was voted by the greatest Number. That the sheriffe should say 'cry "Stephens" as long as you will, he shall never have it'. That he brake of the pole & adiourned the Court 13 myles off. That he would appoynt 7 in the morning & come not till 10. Two in the afternoone & come not till 4. **p.201**

[1]*Resolved*, upon the Question, That in the Opinion of this House, grounded upon the whole Report now made by Mr. *Jones*, Mr. *Harding* and Mr. *Seymor* are well elected, and well returned, and ought to serve in this House' (28 April, *C.J.*, II, p.15).
[2]Possibly Sir Edward Bishop. See above, **p.165**.
[3]See below, **pp.208–211**.

[Committee Reports, 18 April: elections (privileges)]

The 18th day [of April] at Committee of Elections.

Mr. Thurland established at reading Indentures wheere 3: were returned. Mr. Duck[1] & Mr. wyndham[2] for mynheard [Minehead, Somerset], mr. Alexander pophem[3] returned after. Election made by the Constable & the Electors. The electors the other day without the Constable & the Electors another returne. **p.202**

[Committee Reports, 20 April: religion]

Munday the 20th [of April] in the afternoone.

Mr. Crewe in the chayre for the Committee of Religion.

Dr. Farmero.
Questioned for examing by the oath *ex officio*.[4] As hee came in was suddenly examined & confessed hee had given it & excommunicated him that refuzed it.

Mr. Flood.
If hee had, had more time wee had, had lesse truth, *habemus Confitentem reum*: Great vehemence against him exprest by the house.

Dr. Farmero.
Prayes theyr favourable opinion, that hee is not a man rigorous in this busines. Prayes time to recollect himselfe.

Many move for a report of it to the house to morrowe.

Mr. Hambden.
Makes a doubt whether wee have power to report to the house to morrowe.

[1]Arthur Ducke (Minehead). *D.NB; MofP.*
[2]Francis Windham (Minehead). *MofP.* Edmund Windham sat for Bridgwater. *D.NB; MofP.*
[3]Alexander Pophem (Bath). Pophem was returned for both Minehead and Bath. *D.NB. MofP.* 'Mr. *A. Popham* chooses for *Bath*, and waves *Mynhead*' (16 April, *C.J.*, II, p.3).
[4]Farmery was chancellor of the diocese of Lincoln. He was later accused of blackmailing French and Dutch Protestant refugees who had settled in Axholme. See Clive Holmes, *Seventeenth Century Lincolnshire* (Lincoln, 1980), p.60.

Mr. Glynn.
Houlds it iust that hee should have time.

Mr. Moreton.
Would have the same favour to members as to strangers, to surprize noe member but to give him time.

Doctor Farmero.
Denyed the sending out of any excommunication, but the Rule of the Court was to pronounce excommunicate.

Query. Some rayzed a doubt whether this were fitt for this Committee, or for the Court of Iustice.

p.203 Mr. Glynn.
That Courts Ecclesiasticall are not within the heads of Courts of Iustice, the Common lawe takes noe notice of them to be Courts of Iustice.

Mr. Bridgman.
Confessio est probatio probata. They are not called Court of Iustice in any statute, but Courts of Records.

This day were many petitions delivered in concerning innovations in religion.

[Committee Reports, 21 April: privileges]

21 April, Tuesday in the afternoone.
Committee of priveledges.[1]
At the Burough of Meronson [*sic* = Beeralston] in devonshire:[2] Theere were three in Competition, Sir Nicholas Slanning; Mr. wise & Mr. Stroud. The question was put to the Burgers if any of them had a voyce for any but one of them three. They answered 'noe'. Then the writt was read & all agreed to choze mr. Stroud for one, of either mr. wise or Sir Nicholas slanning were chosen Knights of the shires they stood for: & Soe adiourned till another Day.

p.204 Mr. wise was after chosen knight for devon. At a 2ᵈday[3] mr. Harris is chosen by 24. Sir Amias Meredeth by 11 & stroud had but 6.[4]

---

[1] Marginal note: 'Mr. Stroud's election'.
[2] See above, **pp.102–103**.
[3] I.e. at a second election.
[4] Cf. above, **p.102.**

Sir Richard Stroud.[1]
Beares witnes that one Reape confessed he had received £X from Sir Nicholas Slanning for his 2 voyces.

Richard Welcomb.
Affirmes the same the day before the day of election, & £12 a yeare as the souldyer had from the castle.

Mr. Harbert.
Would have noe body sitt heere that comes in by Corruption; to give day for hearing.

Mr. Maynard.
That there is noe reazon if one give money, that that should avoyd the others election. The money appears given to him that had noe voyce.

Mr. pymm.
Though he had noe voyce yet if hee had money it was with ill intent.

Sir Nicholas Slanning.
Being examyned whether hee had offred him any money. He answered not for his voyce but to buy somthing of him to enable himselfe to have a voyce.

Mr. Glynn.
Makes a question if a member may desire the Speaker at Committees to aske a witnes a question.

Mr. Harbert.
That wee must Conforme this to the house.

Sir walter Earle.
That at a grand Committee of the house wee may not. But this was lesse then the whole house & theerfore it was usuall. This confirmd by many parlament men.

p.205 Mr. Tempest.
That the election was Completed the 6th of March. That all were called, such excluded as had noe voyce, & elected by all.[2] Then it was first doubted if any election at the 6th of March. 2dly if a Conditionall election, then voyd. 3rdly That it was not taken for an election, for

---

[1] Sir Richard Strode and Richard Welcomb were not MPs.
[2] See above, **p.102**.

the warrant was mistaken, to the Mayor &c when it should have bin
to the Bayliffe & Burgesses & was returned to be renewed the first
day. If the 2ᵈday lost: for he had but 6 voyces.[1] Others sought to
avoyd the Condition as neither precedent nor subsequent. For that
the question was will any man give a voyce to any but: slanning, wise
& stroud. Are you Content Mr. stroud shalbe in the first place.

Mr. wise.
Testifyes a generall declaration.

Mr. Buller.
That if either were chozen Knight of the shire hee should be in the
first place. That the mayor declared to Mr. Harris that hee shuld not
have the first place. But must content himselfe with the 2ᵈbecause Mr.
stroud in the first. If the precedent condition performed then good.
Others that in elections noe condition. The obiection from the warrant
goes to Mayor, Bayliffes & Burgesses wheere noe mayor was, is good.

Mr. Ball.
Not satisfied in the fact if a full election the first day If onely declared
questionable. For if neither of them had bin chozen Knight: doubts
whether hee should have bin one.

p. 206 Mr. Hyde.
That the reazon for our 'I' or 'Noe' may appeare to the house. Out
of a free guyft I may annexe a condition. To an act of Iustice noe
condition to be annexed.

Sir Thomas Witherington.
Fact not satisfyed, lawe cleere, that the condition voyd whether sub-
seq:[*uent*] or precedent.

Mr. Bridgman.
Neither satisfied in Lawe nor fact. For an election must be in present,
not with relation to a time subsequent.

Baber.
Statute of westminster. 1ˢᵗall elections to be Free. If elected the 6ᵗʰ,
the 27ᵗʰis voyd. Formality of election performed.

---

[1] I.e. if the second poll (27 March) is valid, then Strode, polling only six votes on that
occasion, has lost the seat.

Mr. Ball.

If mr. stroud were postively elected, well. If not a conditionall election is not a free election. This is clogd with a Condition.

Mr. Hollis.

At the woorst hee overthrowes his adversaryes. Argument *a maiore ad minus*: if Condition, performed. Hee is then to stand. If Condition annexed it is voted to be voyd.

Conclusion: Soe the vote of the house it is carryed for stroud.[1]

[Committee Reports, 23 April: elections (privileges)]

April 23^d At the Committee of elections.

East Grimsted in Suffolke.[2]

Three stood in Competion. Sir Henry Compton 24. Mr. whyte (13), & mr. Goodwin 14. Whyte waves his election serves for another place. The question was to avoid Goodwyns election, for that Some of his had noe voyces. Some had conveyances made a purpose to give them voyces. Richard Higget & Anthony Booth were ioynt purchazers of one Burgage. **p. 207** Pretence of Inconvenience if one man divid in parcells a burgage & all to have voyces. Hee may sway a towne. A precept to the Bayliffe & Burgesses return'd by the people without the Bayliffe.

Sergeant clearke.

That maiority of voyces should carry it. One seized of a Freehould in right of his wife, hath a voyce. Noe one man by buying 2 Burgages can have 2 voyces. But 20 iount tennants may have 20 voyces. All men right to have free voyces unlesse restrayn'd by the statute. The statute limitts the returnes to be made by Indentures betwixt the sheriffe, Bayliffe & Burgesses. Presidents of divers Indentures with the woords *alis Communitate* not accepted, because the mayor, Aldermen & freemen in a Citty are called the cominalty. A president of a writt directed *Burgensibus et inhabitantibus* 38:H:8, 6:E:6. This swayed not because a writt may be false directed. Others argue that a Burgage made to severall men. It does not enable them, soe one may make 200 voyces. Instanced in representation to an advowson, which graunted to severall men they cannot all present. Wittnes given that onely Burgesses have voyces. Theerfore a returne made *per Burgos et inhabitantes* doe not overthrowe it. Then was produced a Record

---

[1] See above, **p.103**.
[2] Sussex. See above, **p.61**.

directed to the mayor, Burgesses & Commoners, & the Returne made by divers whoe were prooved to by Commoners. Soe it was voted to be carryed by the maiority of voyces & past for Mr. Goodwin. **p. 208**.

[Committee Reports, 28 April: elections (privileges)]

April 28th. Sir Robert Tracyes election.[1]

Allegations that mr. Stephens[2] had more voyces. One Webb:[er?] Heard Sir Humphrey Tracy[3] the sheriffe say Sir Robert Tracy should be one of the Knights. 2 brothers[4] sayd they heard the sheriffe say 'cry "stephens" as long as you will Stephens shall not have it'. That such as Cryed 'Tracy' were dispatched. That he spoke soe softly for stephens the voyces were lost. That when Sir Robert Tracyes Company were thin he rested halfe an howre. That he adiourned till 8 a clock, & came till ten. Afternoone till 2 & came not till 4. That alwayes when Sir Roberts voyces were Thin; Stephens Thick, hee would adiourne the Court. Saturday night adiournes the Court to Winchcomb.[5] That divers Freehoulders cryed 'noe' to the adiournement. That 180: at least signed a Certificate that they would have bin poled. That they were directed to Come to the Castle Greene & dispatched Sir Robert Tracyes, reiected theyrs.[6]

Mr. Fountayne.[7]
That these exceptions were against men not present. That it is not allowable in any Court of Iustice to question any man wheere he cannot make his defence, much lesse heare. That many things were obiected onely to make a noyse which are not mentioned in the

[1]See above, **p.200**. Sir Robert Tracy (Gloucestershire). *MofP*.
[2]Nathaniel Stephens sat for the county of Gloucester in both the 1628 parliament and the Long Parliament. Keeler, pp.47, 350–51. Stephens' attempt to oust Sir Robert Tracy from his seat was unsuccessful. See *CSPD*, 1639–1640, pp.580–83; W. B. Willcox, *Gloucestershire: A Study in Local Government 1590–1640* (New Haven, 1940), pp.35–36; Hirst, p.149.
[3]Sir Humphrey Tracy was sheriff and a relative to Sir Robert. Willcox, *Gloucestershire*, p.35.
[4]Marginal note: 'William Essex, David Essex'.
[5]'. . . but [*Tracy*] adjourned the court, and continued the election to Winchcomb, a poor beggarly town, conveniently situated for his own, but inconvenient for the repair of Mr. Stephens' supporters' (*CSPD*, 1639–1640, p.581).
[6]'This course Stephens protests against, and, as I hear, intends to remedy by complaint in Parliament' (*CSPD*, 1639–1640, p.581). Aston's account of the Gloucestershire election is based on the petition preferred by Stephens. Cf. the account by a supporter of Sir Robert Tracy's in a letter to Peter Heylyn. *CSPD*, 1639–1640, pp.580–83.
[7]Marginal note: 'objection By'. It appears that Fountain did indeed have time to take the seat vacated by Sir John Packington, when the latter chose to sit for Worcestershire. Cf. Keeler, p.179.

Pettion. Soe any man living may be Convinced in his absence. Like-wise many allegations against the sheriffe which were not Complayned of. The Course of Iustice is the Same in all. Reazon should Rule in all. Prayes that they may proceed upon the Petition.

p. 209 Answear to Fountayne. That these things conduce to the election.

Reply: whether soe men that know nothing shalbe convinc'd in that which were never present nor make any defence.

Mr. Hackwell.
Cytes presidents of some sent for.

Fountayne.
Appeales whether upon meere Information of Counsell. Nothing in writing, nothing in Court before them. If the Committee will meddle with it.

Mr. Maynard.
Though particulars not chardged in the petition if wee heare it, it is against men not present; which if it with intention to condemne them, were not fit. But wee tye not our selves to the petition, then wee should have petitions as long as Bills.

Sir Thomas Witherington.
That tis not fit upon generall woords for sundry abuses, to drawe all men into the question for batteryes, affrayes, slanders, killing, wee may send for all the County of Gloucester. That he honors presidents, but they are many times cyted at *libitum* for mens turnes. A president vouched of yorke. Alderman Hoyle sent for, but hee was in the petition.

Mr. Ball.
That mr. maynard was not answeared. Wee meant not to iudge as a Crime, but if any man appearing in an election, shall assault or batter or trouble those whoe come for a party, we may heare & iudge it.

Mr. moreton.
Of opinion that it was not proper if Conceived inducment to the election. Then not possible to seperate them, for then the parties must be Convinced. If a generall chardge tis a good cause of demurrer, in lawe.

Mr. vaughan.
A mistake: That a generall chardge & matter appearing[*ed?*] by witnesses is not all one. Wee looke after it as the Interest of the house. Noe question the party can but make an equall answeare as good as defence. **p.210** 2^d mistake, that if any man have [*sic*] misbehaved himselfe, wee cnnot avoyd the election unlesse the party punished. Conceives as Concernes Sir Robert Tracy. He is clearly defencelesse. But as in the Interest of the house; a party being brought before us in whom misdeameanor in the election will equally Concerne Sir Robert Cooke.

Sir Thomas witherington.
If it fell in matter of the election fitt to heare it but as casuall: Though Counsell state things at lardge wee may pare them. Which Resolved that wee should examyne as farr as tends to the election.

Proofes[1]: That Captain Bathhurst, threatned him if hee did not give his voyce with him he would make him goe to yorke. Cald one 'cropeard knave' that said hee was for stephens & struck him. That Richard Cutts a page to Sir Robert Tracy struck mr. Stephens with a stick. Mr. George a Iustice threatned one Thomas Taylor a glover saying he thought hee would not have bin against him, but for that trick the towne should have noe releefe for the poore.

Mr. Fountayne.
Answer: That theere was little allyance more than name in Tracy & the Sheriffe. That severall things obiected. 1st a great Cry of Free-houlders, then a bad returne. That they had noe witnesses of woorth. That theyr principall witnes concluded against Sir Robert Cooke, that Tracy had more than Cooke & stephens. 2. They sayd that wheere they stood they heard more voyces for Stephen[*s*]. **p.211** The greatest exception is what these 2 essexes sayd:[2] which if two such, should say hee now fell woords that were Treazon. The Iustification of this assembly hee hopes would cleare him in any Court of Iustice. And mr. stephens part Confessed hee watch'd his woords & heard it not, nor noe wittnes ells. If the sheriffe had not adiourned the Court then the election must stand as it did on Saturday night. The pretence was made of an unfitt place: The Company soe vehement they thronged upon him & overthrewe the Table that they went into a house. That he gave a poore old man the booke whoe was ready to

---

[1]It is unclear in the manuscript whether or not this evidence is given by Sir Thomas Widdrington, by another MP, or by more than one witness.

[2]See above, **p.208**. The evidence in the manuscript suggests that Fountain is answering the allegations made against Sir Humphrey Tracy.

faint. That he sate still a whyle & did nothing was because hee could neither speake nor heare. That when hee adiourned it till six & came not till Ten was sick. That in the afternoone apoynted 2 came not till 4, was because Stephens & his party mayntayned argument that a Lessee for yeares determinable upon lives should have voyces. That for adiourning to Winchcomb they had but winstons testimony, whoe cutt his Beard to goe be pol'd agayne. That he left of earlyer because hee had 15 myle home [*sic*]. That the place was as Convenient. That he must adiourne 5 myle if at all because soe farr is within the Citty. If noe adiournement could be, nor returne, then both voyd. If an error twas not *pravae dispositionis*, they confesse was advised hee might doe it. Either it was compleated or not at reading the writt. If it were they were to goe to tryall upon that. If not then they had the maior part by the poll.

Mr. Hearne.
That the question of Lessees for yeares was press'd soe far that Mr. Stephens sayd hee would proceed noe further.

p.212 Mr. Chadwell's election: St. michells in Cornwall.[1] Three were returned by the Indentures. Wheerof Mr. Chadwell was one. Mr. Bassett excepts that the warrant came to be chozen presently. That 11 signed the Indenture. 4 Almesmen, the messenger, & one from woorke set his hand. Exception taken to suddain elections. The writt was delivered to the port Reave. Hee in person Summoned all but 5. Left notice at theyr houses & they appeared at the place apoynted. Theere were but 19 sworne Burgesses in all, 14 appeare. All inhabitants consent. Cominalty to be interpreted as usually taken either for all, or for the free Burgers. Almes Men that have bin free Burgers to have voyces.

Sir Thomas witherington.
Returne good in respect of the electors. *Liberi Habitantes:* 2ly *prepositus et communitas*, which is the Corporation. Common use makes a Lawe & overthrowes Common right.

Put to the Question & resolved for chadwell.

---

[1]See above, **p.60**.

[Committee Reports, 29 April?: grievances]

Wednesday afternoone.[1] Committee of Greivances. To proceed upon Greivances, of monopolies in theyr order.

Mr. Belleses.
That Yorkshire represented ship money for a greivance from the County.[2]

Mr. vaughan.
Would have every man give his name that did present it from any County.

Mr. Waller.
To put it to the question whether it were thought a greivance by all the Boroughs & Countyes of England & as many as were of that mynd say 'I', those whoe were of another say 'Noe'.

This was the day voted by the whole Committee as Complayned of to be a Greivance by all the Kingdome.[3] **p.213**

[Committee Reports, 29 April: grievances]

April 29th: At the Committee of Greivances.

The post masters pattent complayned of & ordered to be brought in. The feltmakers Complayne of the Beavermakers. That they gave 12[d] upon a Hatt: gett a pattent & a proclamation. The Beavermakers pretend difference in theyr woorkes. That the felt makers abuz'd by mixing. Full of Cozenage. Mix 5s an ounce & 4d togather. That the King lost the benefitt of Imposition of Beaver And had 12d on a Hatt in liew of it.

Mr. Hales.
2°Iac was the first Corporation of felt makers. Noe use of Beavers then: Freemen & forreigners then divided. Mayor could not prohibit abuses. Drew the prizes as High mixt as pure. The felt makers oppose it as part of theyr trade, The materiall not one, fur & wooll, offer of 3 feltmakers make a Beaver to yeild. That what was before £5 was now £3.

---

[1]Probably Wednesday, 29 April.
[2]See above, **p.194**.
[3]See the debates about ship money on 30 April and 4 May (above).

Mr. Chuite.

For the feltmakers that was a trade since civility came in. 30 men severed themselves & drawe the trade which is the great trade now. That there was a contrast before the pattent of £5000 given. That they give oath to pooremen, a warrant dormant to take away such as they make at any time. That they may afford for 3 what for £5 a litle one for a great one. To the Instances of severall Corporations, of whyte bread & Browne, wax & tallow chandelors.

Answer: why not severall Corporations to make Spanish leather & neates leather Bootes, Ioyners for deale & Home boards. Severall wittnesses produced that by theyr pattent they had taken away divers of theyr goods And kept them under messengers hands. Referred till another day.

APPENDIX A

A list of the sources which complement Aston's diary for each day.

Monday, 13 April

Aston's account of the proceedings of 13 April is limited. Cope, pp.53–54, 95–96, 105, 115–23, 223, 244; *C.J.*, II, p.3; *L.J.*, IV, pp.45–49; Nalson, I, pp.306–312; Rushworth, III, pp.1114–20.

Wednesday, 15 April

Cope, pp.55–57, 97, 106, 123–34, 211, 229–30, 244; *C.J.*, II, pp.3–4; *L.J.*, IV, pp.49–54; Nalson, I, pp.312–18; Rushworth, III, pp.1121–27.

Thursday, 16 April

Cope, pp.107, 134–45, 212–15, 233–34, 245, 248–53, 296–98; *C.J.*, II, pp.3–4; Nalson, I, pp.318–22; Rushworth, III, pp.1127–31.

Friday, 17 April

Cope, pp.145–57, 212–13, 216–19, 234–35, 245, 254–60, 275, 298–302; *C.J.*, II, pp.4–6; Rushworth, III, pp.1119–20, 1131–36.

Saturday, 18 April

Cope, pp.158–62, 220, 235, 260–62, 275–79, 302–303; *C.J.*, II, p.6; *Life*, I, pp.72–74.

Monday, 20 April

Cope, pp.162–63, 220, 235, 238n.2, 245–46, 262–63; *C.J.*, II, pp.6–7; Rushworth, I, App. I, III, pp.1136–37.

Tuesday, 21 April

Cope, pp.163–64, 199–220, 235–36, 246; *C.J.*, II, pp.7–8. The afternoon of 21 April was spent in conference with the Lords at the Banqueting House. Cope, pp.66–67, 108–109, 164–67, 199–220, 230–31, 246, 263; *L.J.*, IV, pp.62–63; Nalson, I, pp.333–36; Rushworth, III, pp.1137–39. For a discussion of the assorted texts of the Lord Keeper's speech, see Cope, pp.303–305.

Wednesday, 22 April

Cope, pp.109, 167–69, 201, 221, 236, 246, 280–82; *C.J.*, II, pp.8–9; Rushworth, III, pp.1140–44.

Thursday, 23 April

Cope, pp.169–74, 200, 221–23, 237, 246, 290, 308–310; *C.J.*, II, pp.9–10; Nalson, I, p.330.

Friday, 24 April

Cope, pp.174–76, 223–24, 228–29, 237, 247, 284, 308–310; *C.J.*, II, pp.10–12; Nalson, I, pp.330–33; *CSPD*, 1640, pp.370–71.

Saturday, 25 April

Cope, pp.81, 101, 176–77, 201–203, 231–32, 238, 247, 265–66; *C.J.*, II, p.12.

Monday, 27 April

Cope, pp.177–80, 224–25, 231–32, 238–39, 247, 310–11; *C.J.*, II, pp.13–14; Nalson, I, pp.333–36; Rushworth, III, pp.1144–47.

Tuesday, 28 April

Cope, pp.83, 180, 182–85, 225–26, 227n.2, 239–40, 312–13; *C.J.*, II, pp.14–15; *L.J.*, IV, pp.71–72.

Wednesday, 29 April

Cope, pp.180–82, 203–204, 225–27, 240–41, 266, 313–14; *C.J.*, II, pp.15–16.

Thursday, 30 April

Cope, pp.112, 184–85, 227, 241, 285–87; *C.J.*, II, pp.16–17; Nalson, I, p.337; Rushworth, III, p.1149.

Friday, 1 May

Cope, pp.92–93, 103, 114, 185–87, 204–206, 241–42, 265–72, 287–88; *C.J.*, II, pp.17–18; *L.J.*, IV, pp.75–77; Nalson, I, pp.337–40.

Saturday, 2 May

Cope, pp.114, 187–93, 206–208, 227–28, 242, 273–74, 288–89, 290–91, 316; *C.J.*, II, pp.18–19.

Monday, 4 May

Cope, pp.104, 193–97, 208–210, 243; *C.J.*, II, p.19; Nalson, I, pp.341–42; Rushworth, III, p.1154.

Tuesday, 5 May

Cope, pp.95, 104–105, 114, 197–98, 210, 229, 243–44, 316–18; *C.J.*, II, p.19; *L.J.*, IV, p.81; Rushworth, III, pp.1154–55; Nalson, I, pp.342–43; *CSPD*, 1640, pp.153–54; B. L. Thomason Tracts E. 203 (1), pp.42–47.

Committee Reports

16 April: privileges

C.J., II, pp.3, 6, 7.

20 April: religion

Cope, pp.275–79; *C.J.*, II, p.9.

21 April: privileges

C.J., II, pp.14, 15.

23 April: privileges

None.

28 April: elections (privileges)

C.J., II, p.10.

29 April: grievances

None.

APPENDIX B

CHALMLEY, Sir Hugh, Sir Hugh Cholmley (Scarborough); Keeler; *DNB*. **20, 22, 67, 72, 122, 146, 181, 183, 192**.
[CHOLMEY. See Chalmley.]
CHUITE, mr. Unidentified. Possibly the lawyer Challoner Chute appearing as counsel. *DNB*. **213**.
+CLEARKE, Sergeant. Possibly John Clerke (Rochester); *MofP*. **207**.
[COLEPEPER. See Culpepper.]
[COMBE. See Coomes.]
CONTROWLER, mr. Comptroller of the Household. **9, 20, 22, 34, 37, 42, 50, 52, 57, 66, 68, 90–91, 97, 123, 128, 151, 153, 171, 178, 181, 191**. See also German.
[COOKE, Sir Edward. Probably Sir Robert Cooke.]
+COOKE, mr. Either Henry Coke (Dunwich) or Thomas Coke (Leicester); Keeler; *MofP*. **86, 99**.
COOKE, Sir Robert. Sir Robert Cooke (Gloucestershire); Keeler **43, 94, 154, 169, 182[4], 210**.
+COOMES, mr. William Combe (Warwickshire); Nalson, I, p.300. **153**.
+COWCHER, mr. John Cowcher (Worcester); Keeler. **76, 119**.
+CRADOCK, mr. Matthew Cradock (London); Keeler; *DNB*. **78**.
CRANE, Sir Robert. Sir Robert Crane (Sudbury); Keeler. **98, 152, 171, 178**.
CREWE, mr. Sir John Crew (Northamptonshire); Keeler; *DNB*. **29, 33, 37, 57, 67, 123, 133, 146, 202**.
CRISPE, Sir Nicholas. Sir Nicholas Crispe (Winchelsea); Keeler; *DNB*. **132**.
+CULPEPPER, Sir John. Sir John Colepeper (Rye); Keeler; *DNB*. **6, 99, 106, 126, 130, 181, 183**.
[DANVERS. See Davers.]
DAVERS, Sir John. Sir John Danvers (University of Oxford); *DNB*. **26, 31, 104, 198**.
[DAVIS, Sir John. See Davers.]
[DELL. See Den.]
DEN, mr. William Dell (St. Ives); *MofP*. **41, 42**.
DIGBY, Lord. George, Lord Digby (Dorset); Keeler; *DNB*. **25, 57, 67, 77, 100, 126, 173, 187, 192, 193, 194**.
[DYETT, mr. Probably Sir Richard Dyott. See Dyer, Sir Richard.]
+DYER, Sir Richard. Sir Richard Dyott (Lichfield); *AO*; *MofP*. **25, 43, 121**.
EARLE, Sir Walter. Sir Walter Erle (Lyme Regis); Keeler. **14, 21, 23, 24, 29, 30, 32, 38, 39, 42, 43, 46, 50, 53, 57, 63–64, 67, 68, 75, 79, 80, 87, 96, 101, 107, 114, 117–18, 122, 126, 139, 155, 156, 172, 179, 180, 186, 189, 191, 204**.

+EDEN, Dr. Thomas Eden, Ll.D. (University of Cambridge); Keeler; *DNB*. **120, 127, 150, 153, 164**.

[ERBY, Sir Anthony. See Irby.]

+EVELIN, Sir John. Sir John Evelyn (Ludgershall); Keeler. **138, 193**.

FALKLAND, Lord. Lucius Carey, Viscount Falkland (Newport, Isle of Wight); Keeler; *DNB*. **17, 119, 120, 127, 172, 189, 192**.

FANSHAWE, Sir Thomas. Sir Thomas Fanshawe (Hertford); Keeler; *DNB*; Nalson, I, p.275. **129**.

+FARMERO, Dr. John Farmery, Ll.D. (Lincoln); *AC*; *MofP*. **78, 80, 127, 202**.

+FINES, mr. Either James Fiennes (Oxfordshire) or his brother Nathaniel (Banbury); Keeler; *DNB*; *MofP*. **59, 62, 138, 174, 190**.

+FLOOD, mr. Francis Lloyd (Carmarthen); Keeler; *MofP*. **43, 57, 120, 124, 190, 202**.

[FLOYD, mr. See Flood.]

FLEETWOOD, Sir Miles. Sir Miles Fleetwood (Hindon); Keeler. **21, 26, 44, 97, 186**.

+FOUNTAYNE, mr. Thomas Fountain (Aylesbury); Keeler; *MofP*. **208, 209, 210**.

+FYNCH, mr. Sergeant. John Finch, Serjeant-at-Law (Winchelsea); Keeler. **62**.

[FYNES. See Fines.]

+GEORGE, mr. John George (Cirencester); Keeler. **131, 154**.

GERMAN, Sir Thomas. Sir Thomas Jermyn (Bury St. Edmunds); Keeler. **121**. See also Controwler, mr.

GERRARD, Sir Gilbert. Sir Gilbert Gerrard (Middlesex); Keeler. **14, 115, 181**.

GLANVILL, Sergeant. Sir John Glanville, Serjeant-at-Law, Speaker of the House of Commons (Bristol); *DNB*. **182, 182[4]–83, 183, 188–89, 191, 193**. See also Speaker, mr.

GLYNN, mr. John Glynne (Westminster); Keeler; *DNB*. **18, 22, 24, 26, 42, 52, 72, 74, 78, 90, 99, 100, 143–44, 154, 177, 178, 188, 193, 202, 203, 204**.

GODBOLT, Sergeant. John Godbolt, Serjeant-at-Law (Bury St. Edmunds); *DNB*. **26, 53, 171, 187, 191**.

+GODFREY. Thomas Godfrey (Rumney); Nalson, I, p.300. **63, 78**.

+GOODWIN, mr. Arthur Goodwin (probably Buckinghamshire); or Ralph (Ludlow); or Robert (East Grinstead); Keeler; *DNB*. **37, 61, 62, 169, 175, 180, 190, 193**.

+GOODWYNN of Northampton. Unidentified. **62**.

[GOODWYN. See Goodwin.]

GRIMSTON, Sir Harbottle. Sir Harbottle Grimson (Essex); Keeler; *DNB*. **15, 51**.

GRYMSTON, mr. Harbottle Grimston (Colchester); Keeler; *DNB*. **4, 19, 23, 27, 42, 54, 88, 133, 134, 180, 193**.

+ HACKWELL, mr. Possibly William Hakewill who sat for Amersham in 1628–29, but does not appear in lists of MPs for the Short Parliament. He may be appearing here as counsel. *DNB*; *AO*. **209**.

+ HALES, mr. Probably Sir Edward Hales (Queensborough); Keeler; *MofP*. **213**.

HAMBDEN, mr. John Hampden (Buckinghamshire); Keeler; *DNB*. **17, 19, 27, 31, 32, 34, 38, 41, 42, 53, 56, 58, 63, 65, 67, 69, 75–76, 77, 86, 100, 101, 106, 114, 119, 124, 129, 132, 139, 147, 148, 149, 154, 156, 169, 179, 184, 185, 190, 191, 193, 200, 202**.

+ HAMMON, Sir Peter. Sir Peter Heyman (Dover); Keeler; *DNB*; Nalson, I, p.300. **21, 27, 58, 80, 89, 130, 146, 178, 187, 194**.

[HAMPDEN. See Hamden.]

HARBERT, mr. Edward Herbert, Solicitor General (Old Sarum); or Richard Herbert (Montgomeryshire); Keeler; *DNB*. **19, 21, 22, 25, 27, 29, 30, 40, 41, 44, 52, 53, 57, 58, 67, 69, 75, 87, 96–97, 98, 100, 101, 139, 146, 155, 176, 190, 192, 204**. See also Solicitor, mr.

[HARL. See Harlowe.]

HARLOWE, Sir Robert. Sir Robert Harley (Herefordshire); Keeler; *DNB*. **18, 28, 30, 39, 57, 67, 77, 80, 94, 120, 126, 143, 155, 177, 182[4], 193**.

+ HAZELRIG, Sir Arthur. Sir Arthur Hesilrige, or Haselrig (Leicestershire); Keeler; *DNB*. **54**.

+ HEARNE, mr. Possibly Edward Herle (Bossiney, Tintagel); *MofP*. **211**.

[HERBERT. See Harbert.]

[HERLE. See Hearne.]

[HESILRIGE. See Hazlrig.]

[HEYMAN. See Hammon.]

HOLBOURNE, mr. Robert Holborne (Southwark); Keeler; *DNB*. **26, 39, 43, 64, 91–92, 126, 144–45, 181**.

+ HOLLIS, mr. Denzil Holles (Dorchester); or Gervase Holles (Great Grimsby); Keeler; *DNB*; *MofP*. **98, 101, 107, 124, 147, 154, 190, 206**.

HOPTON, Sir Ralph. Sir Ralph Hopton (Somerset); Keeler; *DNB*. **17, 39, 41, 47–49, 61, 66, 68–69, 76, 99, 106, 121, 131, 151, 156, 187, 193**. See Hutton, Sir Ralph.

+ HOSKINS, mr. Edmund Hoskins (Blechingly); *MofP*. **182[4]**.

HOTHAM, Sir John Hotham (Beverley); Keeler; *DNB*. **14, 32, 65, 69, 72, 76, 91, 98, 101, 106, 117, 126, 129, 147, 176, 180, 182[4], 193, 194**.

+ HUTTON, Sir Ralph. Unidentified. Possibly Sir Ralph Hopton. **45**.

HYDE, mr. Edward Hyde (Wootton Bassett); Keeler; *D.NB.* **15, 19, 33, 53–54, 62, 94, 119, 130, 175, 189, 206**.

+ IRBY, Sir Anthony. Sir Anthony Irby (Boston); Keeler. **121, 127**.

[JERMYN. See German.]

JONES[1], mr. Charles Jones (Beaumaris); or Gilbert Jones (Wareham); or Richard Jones (Radnor); *MofP*; Cope, p.159n.7. **17, 19, 26, 41, 55, 60, 72, 87, 93, 102–103, 104, 134, 145, 150, 152, 165, 176, 184–85, 185, 194**.

KEEPER, The Lord. John, Baron Finch of Fordwich. *D.NB.* **3, 34, 81–84, 156–62**.

KERTON, mr. Edward Kirton (Milborne); Keeler. **14, 18, 21, 27, 37, 50, 55, 94, 101, 114, 129, 139, 166, 171, 181, 189, 191**.

+ KING, mr. Richard King (Weymouth and Melcombe Regis); Keeler; *MofP.* **46, 54, 59, 79, 140, 149, 164, 178**.

KING. The King's Speech. **195–96**.

[KIRTON. See Kerton.]

+ KNIGHTLEY, mr. Richard Knightley (Northampton); Keeler; *D.NB.* **16**.

LENTALL, mr. William Lenthall (Woodstock); Keeler; *D.NB.* **24, 29, 46, 102, 127, 130, 134, 146**.

LEWKENER, mr. Christopher Lewknor (Chichester); Keeler. **20, 24, 27, 45, 67–68, 192**.

LITLETON, Sir Thomas. Sir Thomas Littleton (Great Wenlock); Keeler. **128**.

LITTON, Sir William. Sir William Lytton (Hertfordshire); Keeler. **15**.

[LLOYD. See Flood.]

[MAINWARING. See Manwaring.]

+ MALLARY, mr. William Mallory (Ripon); Keeler. **51**.

MANWARING, Sir Phillip. Sir Philip Mainwaring (Morpeth); *D.NB.* **44, 55, 67, 165, 191, 192**.

MARTIN, Sir Henry. Sir Henry Marten (St. Ives); *D.NB.* **56**.

[MASSALL, mr. See Vassell.]

MASSAM, Sir William. Sir William Masham (Colchester); Keeler. **68, 75, 94, 101, 107, 120, 185**.

MAYNARD, mr. John Maynard (Totnes and Newport); Keeler; *D.NB.* **29, 59–60, 62, 73, 132, 133, 144, 146, 151, 200, 204, 209**.

MILDMAY, Sir Henry. Sir Henry Mildmay (Maldon); Keeler; *D.NB.* **6, 26, 44, 77, 98, 122, 155, 175**.

+ MORETON, mr. William Moreton (Evesham); *AC*; *MofP.* **202, 209**.

---

[1] A. H. Dodd, 'Welsh Opposition Lawyers in the Short Parliament', *Bulletin of the Board of Celtic Studies* (1948), pp.106–107.

MOUNTAGUE, mr. William Montagu (Huntingdon); *DNB*; *MofP*. **178**.

+MOUNTFORD, Sir. Sir Edmund Moundeford(Norfolk); Keeler. **120, 181**.

+NERBON, mr. Probably Simon Norton (Coventry); Keeler; *MofP*. **152, 163, 164**.

NORTH, Sir Roger. Sir Roger North (Eye); Keeler. **29, 131, 168**.

[NORTON. See Nerbon.]

+PALMES, Sir Guy. Sir Guy Palmes (Rutland); Keeler; *MofP*. **87, 114**.

PARREY, Dr. George Parry, Ll.D. (St. Mawes); *MofP*. **167–68**.

PEARD, mr. George Peard (Barnstaple); Keeler; *DNB*. **52, 53, 78, 99, 103, 120, 124, 130, 135–38, 149, 150, 154**.

+PELLAM, mr. Henry Pelham (Grantham); Keeler. **54, 61, 149**.

+PEPS, mr. Richard Peyps (Sudbury); *AC*; *MofP*. **193**.

+PERSEY, mr. Henry Percy (Portsmouth); Keeler; *DNB*; *MofP*. **55**.

[PERT, mr. See Peard.]

PICKERING, Sir Gilbert. Sir Gilbert Pickering (Northamptonshire); Keeler; *DNB*. **14**.

+POOLE, Sir Nevill. Sir Neville Poole (Malmesbury); Keeler. **125, 178, 181**.

PRYCE, mr. Charles Price (Radnorshire); or Herbert Price (Brecon borough); Keeler; *MofP*. **58, 66, 77, 106, 131, 166, 184**.

+PURFRAY, mr. William Purefoy (Warwick); Keeler; *DNB*. **38, 163**.

PYMME, mr. John Pym (Tavistock); Keeler; *DNB*. **6, 9, 10–14, 17, 18, 19–20, 22, 23, 24, 27, 28, 30, 31, 32, 33, 37, 38, 39, 42, 46, 53, 55, 57, 58, 62, 64, 66, 67, 68, 69, 72, 73–74, 75, 77, 79, 80, 86, 89–90, 97, 100, 106, 106–107, 108–109, 109–113, 119, 121, 122, 124, 125, 126, 127, 128–29, 129, 138, 140, 146, 147, 148, 149, 152, 153, 154, 156, 165, 166, 170, 178, 180, 188, 191, 194, 204**.

[RIDDLE. See Ruddle.]

RIGBY, mr. Alexander Rigby (Wigan); Keeler; *DNB*. **14, 28, 59, 102, 130, 134–35, 143, 155, 181, 183, 191**.

+ROBERTS, mr. Unidentified. **50**.

ROWSE, mr. Francis Rous (Truro); Keeler; *DNB*. **9, 44, 120, 149**.

+RUDDLE, Sir Peter. Sir Peter Riddle (Newcastle-upon-Tyne); Nalson, I, p.279. **4**.

RUDYAR, Sir Benjamin. Sir Benjamin Rudyerd (Wilton); Keeler; *DNB*. **5, 46, 89, 99, 124, 180**.

+RUMZEY, . Walter Rumsey (Monmouthshire); *DNB*. **151, 153, 164**.

ST. JOHN, mr. Oliver St. John (Totnes); Keeler; *DNB*. **23, 25, 27, 40, 74, 95, 105, 119, 124, 129, 140–43, 146, 167, 181, 186, 187, 189, 191**.

+ SAVILL, Sir William, Sir William Savile (Yorkshire); Keeler. **194**.
SECRETARY, mr. **16, 28, 32, 54, 57, 140, 175, 188**. See also Windebank.
SEYMOR, Sir Francis. Sir Francis Seymor (Wiltshire); Keeler; *DNB*.
5, 6, 17, 25, 49, 96, 148, 155, 168, 181–82.
SLANNING, Sir Nicholas. Sir Nicholas Slanning (Plympton Earl);
Keeler; *DNB*. **204**. See also Appendix C.
SLINGSBY, mr. Sir Henry Slingsby (Knaresborough); Keeler; *DNB*;
MofP. **192**.
+ SMITH. Sir Thomas. Sir Thomas Smith (Chester); Keeler; *MofP*.
59.
SOLICITOR, mr. **33, 51, 106, 107, 155, 179, 185–86, 187, 193, 194**.
See also Harbert.
SPEAKER, mr. **1, 2, 5, 7, 8, 29, 33, 34, 53, 58, 62, 73, 78, 79, 80, 96,
107, 114, 117, 119, 124, 129, 130, 133, 138, 166, 189**. See also Glanvill.
STRANGEWAYS, Sir John. Sir John Strangways (Weymouth);
Keeler. **16, 27, 31, 43, 44, 50, 72, 120, 130, 154, 177, 182[A], 194**.
STROUD, mr. William Strode (Beeralston); Keeler; *DNB*. **156, 168,
187, 192**.
+ SUCKLING, Sir John. Sir John Suckling (Bramber); *DNB*. **174**.
+ TEMPEST, mr. Unidentified. **205**.
+ THURLAND, mr. Edward Thurland (Reigate); *DNB*; **201**.
+ TOMKINS, mr. Thomas Tomkins (Weobley); or his brother
William (Weobley); Keeler. **103, 117**.
TREASURER, mr. **18, 24, 30, 32, 35, 41, 44, 51, 53, 68, 69, 72, 76,
98, 107, 109, 121, 139, 155, 165–66, 169, 173, 177, 179, 180, 181,
183, 187, 189, 190, 193, 194**. See also Vane.
+ TWISDEN, Sir Roger. Sir Roger Twysden (Kent); *DNB*. **27, 194**.
+ UPTON, mr. John Upton (Clifton-Dartmouth-Hardness); Keeler;
MofP. **119**.
VANE, Sir Henry Vane the elder, Secretary of State, Treasurer of
the Household (Wilton); Keeler. **6, 21**, [28?]. See also Secretary, mr.
and Treasurer, mr.
VASSELL, mr. Samuel Vassall (London); Keeler. **31, 114, 115, 131**.
VAUGHAN, mr. Henry Vaughan (Carthmarthenshire); Keeler;
DNB. **19, 27, 33, 41, 44, 55–56, 68, 97–98, 99, 119, 124, 126, 129,
138, 147, 167, 179, 187–88, 191, 209–10, 212**.
+ W:. Sir George. Probably Sir George Wentworth of Wentworth
Woodhouse (Pontefract); Keeler. **38**.
[WARTON. See Wharton.]
WALLER, mr. Edmund Waller (Amersham); Keeler; *DNB*. **18, 21,
24, 27, 93, 121, 129, 169, 180, 182[A], 190, 211**.
+ WAYNSFORD, mr. John Wandesford (Hyeth); Nalson, I, p.300.
33, 80, 94, 103, 114, 115, 131, 146, 182, 191.

+ WAYNTWOORTH, mr. Unidentified. **55**.

+ WHARTON, mr. Michael Warton (Beverley); Keeler. **130**.

+ WHYTHEAD, mr. Richard Whitehead (Hampshire); Keeler. **65, 78, 124, 131, 154**.

[WIDDRINGTON. See Witherington.]

[WILDE. See Wyld.]

WINDEBANK, mr. Secretary. Sir Francis Windebank, Secretary of State (University of Oxford); Keeler; *D.NB*. **30, 63**.

+ WISE, mr. Thomas Wise (Devonshire), Keeler. **205**.

[WITH:, Sir Thomas. See Witherington.]

+ WITHERINGTON, Sir Thomas. Sir Thomas Widdrington (Berwick-upon-Tweed); Keeler; *D.NB*. **60, 62, 146, 150, 151, 206, 209, 210, 212**.

WRAY, Sir John. Sir John Wray (Lincolnshire); Keeler; *D.NB*. **24, 50, 106, 120, 127, 156, 176, 182**.

WYLD, mr. Sergeant. John Wilde, Serjeant-at-Law (Droitwich); Keeler; *D.NB*. **19, 26, 42, 56, 99, 145, 189**.

+ WYN, mr. Probably Sir Richard Wynn (Andover); Keeler. **42, 77**.

APPENDIX C

OTHER MEMBERS

A list of the members of the Commons who are mentioned in the text of Aston's diary but do not speak.

A cross indicates that the member does not appear in *Proceedings of the Short Parliament 1640*. Eds. Esther Cope and Willson Coates, Camden 4th ser. xix, 1977. Page numbers refer to the pagination of the original manuscript, which is indicated in the text by bold type.

BISHOP, Sir Edward. Sir Edward Bishop (Bramber). **165, 200.**

+ CHADWELL, mr. William Chadwell (Michael); Keeler. **60, 212.**

+ CHEEKE, Sir Thomas. Sir Thomas Cheeke (Harwich); Keeler. **31.**

COMPTON, Sir. Sir Henry Compton (East Grinstead); *AO*. **61, 206.**

+ DUCK, mr. Arthur Ducke (Minehead); *DNB*; *MofP*. **201.**

GOODWIN, mr. Robert Goodwin (East Grinstead); Keeler. **61.**

+ HARBERT, Sir Henry. Sir Henry Herbert (Bewdley); Keeler; *DNB*. **198.**

+ HARDING, mr. Richard Harding (Great Bedwin); Keeler; *MofP*. **103, 199.**

+ HARRIS, mr. John Harris (Beeralston); Keeler; *MofP*. **102, 103, 204.**

+ PACKINGTON, Sir John. Sir John Pakington (double return for Aylesbury and Worcestershire); *MofP*. **149.**

+ POPHEM, mr. Alexander Pophem (Bath); Keeler; *DNB*. **201.**

+ SEYMOR, Charles. Charles Seymor (Great Bedwin); *MofP*. **103, 199.**

+ SLANNING, Sir Nicholas. Sir Nicholas Slanning (Plympton Earl); Keeler; *DNB*. **102, 203.** See also Appendix B.

+ TRACY, Sir Robert. Sir Robert Tracy (Gloucestershire); *MofP*. **200, 208.**

+ WHYTE, mr. John White (Rye); Keeler. **61, 206.**

+ WYNDHAM, mr. Francis Windham (Minehead); *MofP*. **201.**

APPENDIX D

BILLS PRESENTED

A list of bills presented in the Commons during the Short Parliament.[1]

Bill	Aston page numbers (MS in bold type)	C.J., II	Cope
'An act for Conforming apparell'			
15 April, 1°read	**3**	3	
21 April, 2°read and committed	**29**	8	163, 199
30 April, referred to the same committee as Spanish wool	**131**	17	
'An act read for Recoveryes by infants under 21 by vouchers to be voyd'			
16 April, 1°read	**4**	3	Cf. 134
21 April, 2°read and committed	**29**	8	164, 199, 246
1 May, to be considered at committee on Monday	**149**		
'An act read for preventing inconveniences by occupancy'			
23 April, 1°read		9	
24 April, 2°read and committed	**59–60**	10	
'An act for naturalizing James Boore & Suzana ... his wife & Matthewe his son'			
25 April, 1°read	**78**	12	
'A briefe read of ould Bills not finished against long imprisonment'			
25 May (it is unclear whether this was actually read)	**78**		
'Spanish wooll brought in as drawes downe the trade ... Bill To be read on tuesday'			
25 April, discussed	**78**		
28 April, 1°read		14	
'Cleargy be not in Commission of peace'			
25 April, discussed	**78**		
30 April, 1°read	**130**	16	
'For the ease of the clergy from some lay employments'			
1 May, 1°read		18	273–74

[1]The compilation of this table was greatly aided by the List of Bills compiled by Professor Cope (Cope, p319–20).

Bill	Aston page numbers (MS in bold type)	C.J., II	Cope
'An act touching the poynting of needles'			
27 April, 1°read	**86**	13	177
1 May, 2°read and committed	**149**	17	
'Abuse Compelling executors by the ordinary to dispose the goods'			
27 April, discussed	**86**	13	
29 April, 1°read	**116**	16	
2 May, 2°read and committed	**163–64**	18	
'Bill for reformation of abuses in Ecclesiastical Courts'			
20 April, discussed in committee	**202–203**		
27 April, 1°read	**86–87**	13	
'Fees in High Commission & Ecclesiasticall courts' Probably the same as above			
1 May, 2°read?	**149–51**	17	
'A Bill concerning pressing souldgers'			
27 April, 1°read	**87**		
'A Bill for elections'			
16 April, probably a discussion of this bill in committee	**198**		
28 April, 1°read	**102**	14	
'Act for Reformation of elections'			
29 April, related to the above referred to the Committee for Privileges	**116–17**	16	
'For the better ordering of the office of the Clerk of the Market etc.'			
28 April, 1°read.		14	
'An act to imploy Commutation money to pious uses'			
29 April, 1°read	**115**	16	
2 May, 2°read and committed	**163**	18	
'A Bill to enlarge the Liberty of preaching'			
29 April, 1°read	**115**	16	
'Concerning graunting of Administrations to those that belong not. If any dye intestate . . .'			
29 April, 1°read	**115–16**	16	
1 May, 2°read and committed	**151–52**	17	

Bill	Aston page numbers (MS in bold type)	Cope *C.J.*, II
'A Bill to expemt Salop, Woster, Hereford, Gloster from Iurisdiction of the Marches'		
29 April, discussed & referred to the next day	**117**	16
30 April, 1°read	**130**	16
'divers coppyhould Lands in Lancashire, & a Bill come in'		
30 April, referred to speaker as a private bill[1]	**130**	Cf. 16
'a bill for avoyding suitts at Lawe'		
2 May, 1°read	**163**	18
'An act concerning Nonresidences, many livings or Benefices, taking Farms'		
2 May, 1°read	**163**	18
'[Bill for the Reformation of Religion] apparently not introduced'		See p.320

[1]According to Aston, this bill was referred to the Speaker as a private bill. However, *C.J.* (II, p.16) states it was given its first reading. See above, **p.130**.

APPENDIX E

LIST OF PRECEDENTS

A list of precedents cited in Aston's diary.

Page numbers refer to the pagination of the original manuscript, which is indicated in the text by bold type.

Proceedings in Parliament
Hen.III see Edw.III **p.95**.
E.II see 1 Ric.II **p.93**.
6 Edw.III (*Rotuli Parliamentorun ut et Petitiones et Placita in Parliamento* (London, 6 vols., n.d.), II, pp.66–67). **p.57**.
14 Edw.III (*Rot.Parl.*, II, p.112). **p.5**.
15 Edw.III (*Rot.Parl.*, II, pp.126–34). **p.5**.
17 Edw.III (*Rot.Parl.*, II, pp. 135–45). **p.5**.
22 Edw.III (*Rot.Parl.*, II, pp.200–201). **pp.95, 136**.
23 Edw.III see 22 Edw.III. **p.136**.
25 Edw.III (*Rot.Parl.*, II, p.239). **p.136**.
36 Edw.III (*Rot.Parl.*, II, p.271). **p.76**.
50 Edw.III (*Rot.Parl.*, II, p.322). **p.92**.
50 Edw.III (*Rot.Parl.*, II, pp.324–27). **p.136**.
1 Ric.II (*Rot.Parl.*, II, pp.5, 7). **p.93**.
4 Ric.II (*Rot.Parl.*, II, pp.88–90). **p.93**.
5 Ric.II see 6 Ric.II **p.39**.
6 Ric.II (*Rot.Parl.*, III, p.141). **p.39**.
Hen.IV see 5 Hen.IV **p.189**.
5 Hen.IV (*Rot.Parl.*, III, pp.526–27). **p.189**.
8 Hen.IV see 9 Hen.IV **p.87**.
9 Hen.IV (*Rot.Parl.*, III, p.611). **pp.74, 87, 91, 95, 160**.
21, 22 Hen.IV see 22 Edw.III **p.95**.
2 Hen.V (*Rot.Parl.*, IV, p.22). **p.87**.
15 Eliz. see 35 Eliz. **pp.91, 92**.
18 Eliz. (B.L., Sloane MS.326, fols.33–40; *L.J.*, I, pp.742–43; *C.J.*, I, pp.114–15). **p.99**.
35 Eliz. (S. D'Ewes, *The Journall of all the Parliaments during the Reign of Queen Elizabeth* (London, 1682), pp.480–89). **pp.91, 92**.
7 Jac.I (E. R. Foster, ed., *Proceedings in Parliament, 1610* (New Haven, 2 vols., 1966), II, pp.85–86). **p.182**.
18 Jac.I (*C.D. 1621*, II, pp.330–96; III, pp.105–322; IV, pp.270–380; V, pp.109–180, 353–86; VI, pp.107–171, 397–404; *L.J.*, III, pp.95–132; *C.J.*, I, pp.596–628). **p.75**.
21 Jac.I (*L.J.*, III, p.275; *C.J.*, I, p.679). **p.55**.

4 Car.I (*C.D. 1629*, pp.103–106, 170–72, 239–44, 252–67). **p.19**.

Proceedings in Convocation
2 Jac.I (D. Wilkins, *Magna Concilia* (London, 1737) IV, pp.378–79).
p.66
3 Jac.I see 2 Jac.I **p.66**.
16 Car.I (*Foedera*, XX, pp.403–405). **p.64**.

Statutes
Magna Carta (17 John). **pp.56, 135**.
Charter of the Forest (2 Hen.III). **p.12**.
De Fallagio Non Concedendo (25 Edw.I). **pp.135, 136**.
4 Edw.III, c.14. **pp.13, 75, 76**.
14 Edw.III, stat.1, c.20, 21. **p.135**.
14 Edw.III, stat.2, c.1. **p.135**.
24 Edw.III see 4 Edw.III, c.14. **p.76**.
36 Edw.III, c.10. **pp.13, 75, 76**.
5 Hen.IV, c.6. **p.74**.
11 Hen.IV, c.1. **p.87**.
1 Ric.III, c.2. **p.136**.
21 Hen.VIII, c.13. **p.113**.
25 Hen.VIII, c.19. **p.64**.
25 Hen.VIII, c.21. **p.163**.
1 Edw.VI, c.1. **p.86**.
1 Jac.I, c.17. **p.213**.
2 Jac.I see 1 Jac.I, c.17 **p.213**.
21 Jac.I, c.33. **p.114**.
Petition of Right (3 Car.I, c.1). **pp.23, 135, 137, 141, 145, 188**.

Cases
Francis Bacon (*L.J.*, III, pp.53–55). **p.16**.
Bate (impositions) (*Cobbett's Complete Collection of State Trials* (London, 34 vols., 1809–28), II, pp.371–94). **p.11**.
Duke of Buckingham (*L.J.*, III, pp.570, 576–77; *C.J.*, I, pp.847, 849–52). **pp.16, 43**.
Earl of Dover v. Fox (G.C. Squibb, *High Court of Chivalry* (London, 1959) p.64n). **p.15**.
Eliot, *et al.* (*State Trials*, III, pp.293–310). **p.16**.
George Ferrer's Case (*Holinshed*, III, pp.824–26). **p.74**.
Hampden (shipmoney) (*State Trials*, III, pp.825–1316). **pp.12, 132–33, 189**.
Mompesson's Case (*DNB* under Mompesson, Giles). **p.153**.
Saltpetre Case (E. Coke, *Reports XII*, pp.12–13). **p.189**.
Soap (Starchamber) (Rushworth, II, pp.189–90, 252–53). **p.12**.

Duke of Suffolk (*Rot. Parl.*, V, pp.176–83). **p.16** ('Saffol').
Thomas Thorp's Case (*Rot. Parl.*, V, p.239). **p.74.**

INDEX

acts *see* legislation
Acts and Monuments of Matters happening in the Church (Book of Martyrs), 90
addresses *see under* Charles I, addresses to Parliament; Finch, *Sir* John, *Baron Finch of Fordwich*: Lord Keeper's addresses to Parliament
Alestree *see* Allestry
Algerian pirates, 28
Allestry, William, 34, 77, 163
Altare Christianum, 89 n. 1
altars, 8, 12, 22, 25, 88, 89, 90, 91, 92, 96, 112, 137
annual/frequent parliaments, 10, 12, 58, 59
Antidotum Lincolniense, 89 n. 1
apparel, 2, 23, 99
Arundel, *Earl of see* Howard, Thomas
Ascough *see* Ayscough
Aston, John, xiv
Aston, *Sir* Thomas
    life, xiii–xvi
    speeches in Parliament, 75–6, 103, 143–4, 163
    wine importing business, 10 n. 4
Atkins, Thomas, 12, 163
Attorney General *see under* Bankes, *Sir* John
Aylesbury, 109
Ayscough, *Sir* Edward, 47

Baber, John, 23, 78, 151, 163
Bacon, Francis *First Baron Verulam and Viscount St. Albans*, 13, 178
Ball, Peter, 11, 17, 20, 27, 33, 39, 40, 44, 52, 66, 70, 71, 92, 105, 141, 147, 151, 152, 154, 163
Baltinglas, *Lord see* Roper, Thomas
Baker *see* Baber
Bancroft, Richard, *Archbishop of Canterbury*, 52 n. 2
Bankes, *Sir* John, *Attorney General*, 3
The Bar, 36
Baring, Barington *see* Barrington
Barnardiston (Barneston), *Sir* Nathaniel, 11, 163
Barrington, *Sir* Thomas, 36, 66, 81, 88, 95, 97, 109, 112–3, 163

Barwick *see* Berwick
Basset, Francis, 46, 156
Bastwick, John 109 n. 1
Bastwick, Susanna, 109
Bate, John, 9 n. 1, 24, 56, 178
Bath, 148 n. 3
Bath and Wells diocese, 87
Bathurst, *Captain*, 155
Beale, William, 112–5
beavermakers, 157
Bedwin, 78, 146
Beeralston, 77, 149–52
Belasyse (Bellasis), Henry, 142–3, 157, 163
Belasyse (Bellasis), John, 163
Berralston *see* Beeralston
Berwick, 7
Beverley, 142 n. 1
Bewdley, 146
bills *see* legislation
Bishop, *Sir* Edward, 120, 147, 171
bishops, xiv, 2, 9–10, 64, 93, 95, 131
Blundell, Edward, 47 n. 2
Book of Common Prayer, xv, 11, 88 n. 1, 91 n. 1, 99 n. 1, 138 n. 1
Book of Martyrs, 90
Book of Sports, 7, 8, 54, 87, 94, 112
Boone, Gilbert, 127, 163
Booth, Anthony, 152
Bosvile (Bosevile, Boswel), Godfrey, 92, 163
Bowyer, *Sir* Thomas, 46, 120, 163
Bramber, 120
Bramston, *Sir* John *Chief Justice, Court of King's Bench*, 30, 49, 115, 163
breach of Commons' privileges involved in Lords' vote on supply, 67–76, 79, 81–4, 116–8, 121, 130
Brereton, *Sir* William, xiv
Brerewood (Brerwood), Robert, 35, 163
Bridgeman, Orlando, 18, 33, 111, 119, 123–4, 136, 149, 151, 163
Bristol, *Earl of see* Digby, George
Bromfield, *Sir* Edward, 98
Brownrig, Ralph, 35 n. 2
Brunkard, *Sir* William, 64
Buckingham, *Duke of see* Villiers, George